JUST PLAY LIKE YOU DO IN THE BASEMENT

JUST PLAY LIKE YOU DO IN THE BASEMENT

Coming of Age as the Drummer for the
Greatest Entertainer in the World

A Memoir

Rick Porrello

Next
Hat
Press,
LLC

Next Hat Press, LLC
P.O. Box 23
Novelty, OH 44072
www.rickporrello.com
info@rickporrello.com

Subsidiary rights managed by

Global Lion Intellectual Property Management, Inc.
www.globallionmanagement.com

Cover design by *JD&J Design LLC* and Rick Porrello
Interior design by Arun Lakshmanan and Rick Porrello

Publisher's Cataloging-in-Publication
Provided by *Cassidy Cataloguing Services, Inc.*

Names: Porrello, Rick, author.

Title: Just play like you do in the basement : coming of age as the drummer for the greatest entertainer in the world / Rick Porrello.

Description: Novelty, OH : Next Hat Press, LLC, [2025] | "A Memoir." | Includes bibliographical references and index.

Identifiers: LCCN: 2025907085 | ISBN: 9798987831212 (KDP hardcover) | 9798987831236 (IngramSpark hardcover) | 9798987831243 (trade paperback) | 9798987831250 (ebook)

Subjects: LCSH: Porrello, Rick--Childhood and youth. | Davis, Sammy, Jr., 1925-1990. | Drummers (Musicians)--United States--Biography. | Entertainers--United States--Biography. | Jazz musicians--United States--Anecdotes. | Music trade--United States--History--20th century. | Police--United States--Biography. | Coming of age. | Career changes. | LCGFT: Biographies. | Anecdotes. | BISAC: BIOGRAPHY & AUTOBIOGRAPHY / Music. | BIOGRAPHY & AUTOBIOGRAPHY / Memoirs. | PERFORMING ARTS / General.

Classification: LCC: ML419.P668 A3 2025 | DDC: 782.42165092--dc23

First Edition

To my brother,
Raymond Porrello, Jr.

PHOTOGRAPH ACKNOWLEDGEMENTS

All other photographs are from Porrello family collections except as noted with captions.

"I move from one sound to the next, remembering what I have just sung and expecting what I shall sing next; I am stretched between what I have done and what I shall do."

From *Augustine: The Confessions* by Gillian Clark

ACKNOWLEDGEMENTS

Thank you to Frank Accardo, Terri Adley, Deanna Adams, Susan Cahn, Dean and Sharon Carter, Tracy Carter, Rebecca L. Davis, Tom Dreesen, Matthew Hendricksen, Jo-Ann Hodge, Kathy McKee, Linda Metaxas-Fisher, Lester Mornay, Tony Orlando, Lee Porrello, Gary Raynor, Eygie Rhodes, Susan Porrello Shimooka, Keith Strachan, Ilene Vactor, Versare Café & Market.

Special thanks to my brother, Ray Porrello, Jr., and my friend and editor, Cherie Rohn.

PROLOGUE

I was twenty-one years old in late 1983 when I first had the idea to write this book. I'd just left my role as a drummer—a dream job I'd taken over from my brother Ray two and a half years earlier. It was a dream not just for me but also for our father, who had spent years urging us to follow in his footsteps as jazz drummers.

In the months that followed, two people independently suggested I write about my experiences. I thought:

Yes, I should.

I began jotting down memories and drafting early chapters. But the book was put on hold. Instead, an old curiosity—seeded in childhood—drew me into researching my family's dark and complex history. That journey led to five published books and even a couple of film adaptations. It wasn't until 2021 that I returned in earnest to the story I had originally planned to tell, eventually titled *Just Play Like You Do in the Basement.*

Since I owe so much of my musical path to my brother and father, I started by exploring the family influences that brought me to that job—and eventually led me to walk away from it. What began as a coming-of-age story evolved into something deeper: a look behind the curtain of a traveling entourage and what it meant to live in the orbit of a legend.

Almost all of this book's personal stories and dialogue are based on my memories. My brother's recollections—based on his own time on the road—along with interviews and general research, helped fill in the gaps. I've changed the names of romantic partners and blended traits into composite characters, dramatizing some of those relationships while staying true to their emotional core.

A few lines of dialogue are created for clarity, but the essence of my experiences remains true.

I had the rare privilege of seeing a superstar up close. But writing this memoir helped me understand him—and myself—in a way I never had at the time. It was an unforgettable chapter in my life. Still, I wasn't done chasing dreams.

CHAPTER 1

On Friday, January 16, 1981, I maneuvered past the bass and guitar amplifiers and a monitor as I climbed to the drum riser. I sat stiffly at my drums in preparation for my first rehearsal. Eight mics surrounded my kit—one per drum, one for the hi-hat, and two overhead for the cymbals. While adjusting my drums, I took in the scene. Behind me was the percussionist with his timpani, vibraphone, and congas. To my left, trumpet, trombone and saxophone players were sidestepping into their respective rows and past music stands and instruments to take their seats. The guitarist had a cylindrical device sitting on his amplifier. It had a power cord, but I couldn't immediately tell what it was. To my right were violinists, violists, and cellists. It would be my first time working with strings. And with drum mics. And with a monitor.

The weight of the drum book surprised me as I placed it on my snare drum. I peeled apart the Velcro strap, opened it, and picked through both sides from front to back. There must have been over one hundred arrangements. Most were three to five pages long. My experience was with drum charts that were only one or two pages long. Unfamiliar song titles and lengthy medleys with penciled-in notations and cues jabbed at my waning confidence. There was chatter about the lineup. I glanced to my left. A couple of trombonists were looking at a piece of paper.

Ah, a list of songs. It must be the line-up.

I found my copy on the floor under my stand. The second song was *Every Little Beat Helps*. I was familiar with this fast-paced band feature. It included an extended drum solo.

We're going to do Every Little Beat Helps on my first show?

I took a deep breath and returned to the line-up, which had about twenty songs on it. George Rhodes had come out and was at the conductor's podium looking at music. I tried to play it cool as I double-checked my cymbal stands to ensure each adjustable telescoping section was secure, then returned to my music. A minute later I started looking around again.

The musicians checked the clip-on lights on their stands. Some were warming up—soft, long tones and loud bursts that blended with chit-chat and chuckles. Most players were in their thirties, forties and fifties, no doubt the Minneapolis/St. Paul region's finest and most experienced. They looked so confident—just another day at work. The chatter halted as George started to speak. His voice was soft-spoken and friendly, but it left no doubt that he was clearly in charge.

"After *Every Beat Helps*, the boss will come out, sing his first three songs, then we'll see what he wants to do."

George said something about Bob Melvin, the comedian on the show. But his previous words echoed in my head.

We'll see what the boss wants to do?

Playing an extended solo during my audition gig was an unexpected stressor. Then I learned that the line-up wasn't a list of all the songs in the order we would play them. It was only a pool of songs. Individual tunes would be randomly selected on the fly!

The opening theme song was a laid-back groove called *Murphy*

Here. George counted it off and we started playing. After just eight bars, he cut us off. I thought I did something wrong. "Okay," George said, "let's move on to Every Beat."

We're not going to run through the whole arrangement?

George directed his attention to me. After my solo, he wanted me to play four bars on my hi-hat to bring back the band. Though my jazz orchestra experience mainly was with dance bands, I knew this technique well from listening to the great drummer Louie Bellson. George counted off *Every Little Beat Helps.* "One, Two, Two, And!" The intensity of this group on the up-tempo tune struck me. Such musical firepower! We stopped only twice for my two minor foul-ups. As soon as we finished, I glanced at George, hoping for some acknowledgment that I had performed to his satisfaction. There was none.

We rehearsed more music. In most cases, George had the band play the beginnings, certain sections, and the ending. After another half dozen songs, he called a break. Most of the musicians walked off the bandstand. I stayed at my drums and looked through the tunes that were up next, and recalled my father's advice:

Just play like you do in the basement.

This wasn't just a typical rehearsal. It was the first step in proving I could handle the live shows I was expected to play over the weekend. At eighteen, with only two years of professional drumming behind me, I'd played a few shows—but never for a superstar entertainer.

How did this wild, improbable opportunity all start? Well, it began when I was just a kid.

CHAPTER

2

In the 1970s, if you gave anyone who knew my immediate family a word association test starting with "Porrello," their responses would likely be "drums." Drumming was in our blood—Dad played, my brother Ray played, and I tried to keep up.

I grew up in Cleveland Heights. It remains a large, vibrant suburb with housing that ranges from neat bungalows to various apartment buildings and mansions bordering upscale Shaker Heights. Shopping areas include a half-dozen commercial districts of varying flavors and a major mall. A few synagogues, many churches, and schools—public and private—dot the city. My street, Washington Boulevard, has closely situated single and two-family homes on both sides, except for our block where Cleveland Heights High School's campus takes up the entire side opposite my old house.

I was the youngest of three children. My mother cooked and cleaned. When I was three or four years old, she comforted me during thunderstorms. "That's just God playing the drums."

As the months progressed, watching my favorite television show transformed me. "Look! Up in the sky. It's a bird. It's a plane. . ."

My obsession with *The Adventures of Superman* brought laughs to my family. It started when my mother gave me one of her old kitchen towels. Pressing red and yellow Crayolas to the towel, I drew Superman's "S" in the iconic shield. My own cape! And off I went. "Look! In the living room. It's a bird. It's a plane…"

Superman wasn't the only thing that caught my attention. On weekday mornings, while my mom poured my cereal, I'd find myself drawn to the sound of engines roaring and brakes squealing. I'd always be at the front window, watching the older kids pour off the yellow school buses, ready to start their day.

A blaze orange glove, mounted on a stick like a flag pole on the front of our house, identified it as the home of a "Helping Hand" mom. These volunteer ladies were available to assist lost or otherwise distressed children. My mother's participation in the program was an extension of her caring nature and belief that neighbors should watch out for each other.

When I reached school age, my mother went to work as a department store clerk. After eating my breakfast of *Life* or *Cap'n Crunch* cereal, I'd descend our steep, narrow driveway, often meeting a friend or two for the half-mile walk to elementary school. My most memorable written assessment from a teacher was that I was a classroom "peacemaker." After school, I would spend time outdoors with friends. If not outside, I was probably playing my brother's drums or watching television—probably *Lost in Space, Gilligan's Island* or *I Dream of Jeannie.*

My siblings treated me well—mostly. Music—especially the drums—was the main subject when I spent time with my brother. Occasionally he would take me to Mawby's near the big intersection of Cedar and Lee Roads on the other side of the high school. We would sit at counter stools for a burger and a chocolate malt. My sister, Susan, six years older than me, might take me along to her softball game. I was probably seven when my brother and sister, under the guise of Hide-and-Seek, coaxed me into the darkness of the living room closet. They held the door closed until I cried. Both caught it good from my mother.

Whenever I was teased, Mom would tell me, "Don't let them get your goat."

I understood what she meant, even if I had no idea what my goat was.

Most of my childhood memories are related to music, though one involving hot coffee sticks out. The primary learning and practice setting within our ten-room, three-floor house was in the basement. You got there through the eat-in kitchen between the back entrance to the house and a formal dining room. On one side of the kitchen was the counter with the sink, cupboards above and below, and a chute where you dropped dirty clothing for a one-way flight to Mom's laundry basket.

The other side of the kitchen held a four-seat table and our old gas range. To light the oven, you had to turn on the gas, strike a match, and hold it steadily at the little hole in the bottom of the oven. The quicker you heard a soft WHOOSH, the better. Once you glimpsed a blue flame, you would rotate the dial to adjust the oven temperature. I sometimes wondered why the temperature was adjustable since my mother baked everything at 350 degrees Fahrenheit. Lighting that gas oven without adult supervision, despite my fear that an explosion would level the block, was a rite of passage. For God's sake, light the match first, then turn on the gas.

Next to our range was a door that opened to a stairwell. Descend to enter our dimly lit basement, and you were met by a goliath of a gray furnace. Walk to the right, past a storage closet we called the tool room, and you came to an old upright piano and a vibraphone. They sat just outside an open corner lit up like a stage—the drum room.

The drum set was center stage, but the room also held stereo equipment, Latin percussion instruments, and poorly-stacked record albums. My dad and brother decorated the walls with framed eight-by-ten-inch photographs of musicians and bands. They ranged from local groups to internationally known stars, including Duke Ellington and Frank Sinatra. There were a couple of personalized pictures of Louie Bellson. He figured prominently in my family. And there were older framed photos of my father's jazz combos from many years earlier.

Occasionally my mother sat at the piano and made her way through the sheet music to twenty or so jazz standards. She played the piano for fun, but my family's passion for music began with my father, a descendant of Sicilian immigrants. He came of age in the 1940s during America's swing era. After fleeting interests in accordion, piano, and vibraphone, he settled on the drums. Army service interrupted his music lessons, but his talent as a drummer was recognized, and he was assigned to the 16th Infantry 1st Division Band based out of Fort Bragg, North Carolina. He toured Germany and Austria, playing with small groups and dance bands at officers' clubs. In 1947, he was discharged and returned to Cleveland. As a veteran, he used his G.I. Bill benefits to study at the Cleveland Institute of Music and later joined the musicians' union.

By the mid-1950s, my dad and mom were raising a family. Like most men in his social circle, he was tough and a hard worker. He needed a steady paycheck to care for his family—something more reliable than music. Dad went to barber school, got his license, and eventually opened his own shop. He continued playing the drums on weekend evenings.

Like other major cities, Cleveland had no shortage of live music. Musicians of all stripes gigged regularly at bars, nightclubs, strip joints, country clubs, party centers, yacht clubs, theaters, and jazz clubs. Nationally-known entertainers passed through town and performed at large concert venues like Playhouse Square, Public

Auditorium, and Musicarnival, a tent theater. They played on smaller stages like the Bluegrass Motor Inn and the storied Theatrical Grill.

During this time, my father met Louie Bellson. He was a celebrated drummer, soloist, bandleader and composer. As an innovator he is best remembered for creating the drum set with two bass drums instead of one. Through the years, Louie and my dad became dear friends.

Around 1968, my father became interested in a new officer's position at the musicians' union. It was titled Assistant to the President. He appealed to his Aunt Maggie, a prominent resident of Little Italy who operated a small winery with her husband. They were influential with Tony Milano, the longtime *consigliere* or counselor of the Cleveland Mafia. The mob needed friends in positions of power and authority to operate successfully. They had influential allies in many labor unions, including the smaller ones.

My father got the job. He left barbering and worked at the intersection of live entertainment and organized labor, thus positioned peripherally in the far-flung network of the Cleveland crime family. His responsibilities included reviewing and approving performance contracts between club owners and Local 4 musicians, recruiting young players for the 3,800-member-strong organization, and protecting them from unscrupulous booking agents.

Meanwhile, my brother, Raymond Porrello, Jr., was four or five years old when he took a liking to my father's red sparkle drum set. When Ray could finally balance on the stool, he would hold the sticks and, with my father's encouragement, hit snare, hi-hat, and ride cymbals. Reaching the bass drum and hi-hat pedals would come a little later. But Ray was already hooked. His interest and ability gained steam, but Dad had one stipulation. If Ray wanted to continue playing, he had to take lessons. His first teacher was Ed Bobick, a local small-group drummer who had studied in New York City with nationally recognized percussion instructors and authors.

Ed, a bachelor in his fifties, was small in stature but big in his passion for education.

As my brother's music education progressed, the drum room became a serious place of practice. It might be midnight, but if you stood at the top of the basement stairwell, you could hear the smooth and even tapping of Ray's sticks on a rubber practice pad. As easy as it might seem, making each alternating stroke produce the same sound in a steady tempo was challenging. Often Ray practiced with a metronome, an electric or wind-up device that produces an audible click in perfect time.

During the day, the drum room was an occasional gathering spot for cousins and neighborhood friends with a natural fascination for music. What boy didn't want to play the drums? Girls, too. My brother would play the set while one friend annoyingly assisted and another tried his hands at the bongos, cowbell, or tambourine. Yet another would tap on the tired keys of our piano.

As the years rolled by, we often had visits from relatives. Most of my father's many first cousins were as close as siblings. Perhaps they bonded due to the shared trauma of their childhoods. One of my favorite cousins was Tony. He had a standard question when he telephoned us, and I answered: "Is this the person to whom I'm speaking?" When he came for dinner, Tony insisted I wear a tie at the table. Even if I was wearing a tee shirt, I had to run to my bedroom and return with my clip-on tie. Tony would fasten it to my collar and then inspect the results. "Okay. That's better." He would laugh, and I would eat while wearing a tee shirt and tie.

My father sometimes had Ray play the drums for guests. Showing off his son's talent was an extension of his long-held interest in music. No doubt, nudging Ray forward as a drummer brought my father vicarious pleasure. Dad's blood history couldn't be erased, but his musical aspirations might turn the pages to a brighter family legacy.

My brother was fifteen when Dad took him to the Theatrical Grille, a downtown nightclub frequented by racketeers, attorneys, sports celebrities, and businessmen. The club featured nationally known entertainers, and that evening, drummer Gene Krupa was performing. Krupa became famous during the swing era with Benny Goodman's big band and his floor tom-tom solo on the 1937 hit *Sing, Sing, Sing.* Known for his facial expressions and unique movements, Krupa was one of the first drummers to bring the big band stickman into the spotlight.

After the performance, Dad took Ray backstage to meet Krupa. Not long after, my father similarly introduced Ray to Louie Bellson, who was performing with Tony Bennett. My brother was mesmerized by Louie's sparkling white pearl kit with two bass drums. After the show, Louie invited Ray to help break down the set—and two months later, gave it to him. Over the next few years, Louie also gave Ray cymbals and big band charts—full arrangements for an 18-piece jazz orchestra.

In 1970, Ray was sixteen and started playing local gigs. I was seven years old and banging away on the Bellson set and cymbals in the drum room. When Ray was home, he often coached me.

"Here, listen," he might say, grabbing a stick from me. Then he'd demonstrate the ride cymbal beat.

Keeping time on the ride cymbal is something every young drummer has to get right.

"You were playing it too choppy, Ricky. Smooth it out, like triplets," he'd explain, my head bobbing in agreement.

By then, I used my left hand to hold my fork and throw a ball. I had broken the right-handedness mold in my family. But when it came to the drums, I was more or less forced to play right-handed, which would bode well for me in later years. With coaching from my brother and father, my random clicks, cracks, and crashes turned into coordinated beats and rhythms. By age eight, I was playing along to Louie Bellson's albums.

Whenever Louie appeared in Cleveland, my father invited him for dinner. Mom would prepare an impressive meal. She might start with wedding soup and for a vegetable, serve string beans sprinkled with olive oil flavored with some minced garlic. And for the main course, it was often lasagna and veal cutlets—two Bellson favorites.

During those visits, Dad was truly in his element as he invited Louie and Ray—mentor and protégé—downstairs to take turns at the drum set. I stood quietly behind them, absorbing the sights and sounds, captivated by Louie's dexterity and control.

My brother's learning from one of the greatest drummers in the world!

"Watch out," Louie would warn while gesturing toward me and grinning. "He's gonna steal our licks."

I grinned but said nothing. Louie was right, of course. I watched every move as he and my brother made the drum set come alive.

When I was about ten, Louie spent two nights with us. My mother changed the sheets on my bed and fixed up my bedroom for him. I was thrilled to give it up. I got to sleep on the sofa in our sunroom, which had many windows and served as a television room and office. During the day, Louie might sit at the desk to make phone calls. Out of respect, since he was a guest, he would leave the door open. As a courtesy, my mother would close the doors softly as Louie began his calls. Afterward, he might emerge and say, "Pearl sends her love." Pearl Bailey was a famous black actress and singer. She and Louie had married twenty years earlier when much of society did not accept interracial couples. Louie often served as bandleader and music director for Pearl's nightclub act.

During Louie's downtime, my father might take him to his office at Local 4. A few days after Louie departed Cleveland for his next gig, he sent my parents a postcard filled with gratitude for their hospitality.

***

When my father had to stop at his office, he'd sometimes bring me along. Local 4 of the American Federation of Musicians was in a two-story, light-colored brick building just east of downtown. A giant treble clef with musical notes on the east wall displayed the main number and the slogan, "Call for Live Music." Behind the union, on the next block, was the county juvenile detention home. A block away stood the powerful Teamsters Joint Council 41 headquarters.

Dad and I entered through the rear door, turned right, greeted and passed his secretary, then entered his office. It had bluish plastic blinds facing the parking lot and detention home. His desk was metal. One time I spotted a revolver inside a drawer.

When Dad was on the phone, I'd wander and greet employees. Each year I grew bolder. I started with the secretary, then moved into the president's office. A woodgrain table for eight was just inside the office. Even then, I knew it was where the board of directors met. At the far end was the president's desk. I knew not to bother him if he was on the phone. If he didn't greet me, I'd continue into the lobby, with its grand piano, a few chairs, and two large paintings of musical instruments.

I might run into Bill Lewis, the tall custodian with keys jingling from his belt. He also worked as a locksmith and handyman. From time to time, Dad hired him for repairs at our house. Bill would explain what he was doing and let me help him.

On the opposite side of the lobby, past the piano, was the payroll department. There, the treasurer, a former drummer like Dad, would greet me with a smile and "Ricky!". After a handshake, he'd hand me drumsticks, and we'd trade licks on his desk.

Then, I'd visit the payroll ladies. The highlight was operating the machine that printed and cut the checks. They'd fuss over me, offer candy, or get me a soda from the lobby vending machine before the questions began.

"How is school?"

"Good."

"How old are you now?"

"Eleven."

Are you going to play the drums like your father and brother?

"Yes."

Do you have a girlfriend?"

I told them I didn't have a girlfriend. I did not tell them I had a crush on my new neighbor. It was springtime when Sandy and her boyfriend Bob, both in their mid-twenties, rented space in the house next door. Sandy was tall and slim, had short, curly blonde hair, and wore tight jeans. She caught my eye when she wore her royal blue tank top that swooped under one arm. Or when she wore anything else. It was a time before air conditioning was a common amenity, so most people kept their windows open due to the nighttime heat and humidity of July and August. Sandy and Bob argued often. The houses were close to each other, and their fights were loud enough to be overheard. I listened, hoping that he did not hurt her. But it was soon apparent that they quickly and routinely resolved their differences.

Sandy and Bob didn't have curtains. I knew because my bedroom was directly across from theirs. They had a window shade but seldom lowered it. The late evening action kicked off with the soft red glow of their let's-get-it-on lamp. Shadowy, rhythmic motions and the muffled moans of this swingin' couple's intimate acrobatics followed. My mother often said neighbors should keep an eye on each other.

CHAPTER 3

I was about eight or nine years old when I first overheard that my grandfather had been murdered. It had something to do with the mob. At the time, my understanding of organized crime was limited to watching *The Untouchables* on television with my father. Based on Eliot Ness's memoir, the series was dramatic and thrilling, but my grandfather's death was brutally real—he was killed decades earlier, along with three of his brothers, in separate shootings.

A year later, I was browsing our bookshelf. Among my father's books was *The Mobs and the Mafia*, in which Hank Messick briefly mentioned my grandfather and his six brothers. The bloodshed was tragic, but I was a generation removed from the trauma. I was fascinated. Nobody in my family spoke about the murders, but that would change on my account.

My grandfather, Raimondo (Raymond) Porrello, was the youngest of seven brothers from Licata, Sicily. In the early 1900s, they immigrated with the Lonardo brothers and became partners. The Lonardos were influential figures in the Sicilian-American Mafia, gaining power during Prohibition. At their height, they controlled the wholesale distribution of corn sugar, a key ingredient in liquor distilling.

Then came the bloody Sugar War. By 1930, three Lonardo brothers and two of my great-uncles were dead. The surviving Porrellos, including my grandfather, carried pistols and hired bodyguards. A rumor of revenge led to a deadly confrontation with the more powerful Mayfield Road mob. My grandfather, one of his brothers, and their bodyguard were playing cards when three gunmen stormed in. Shots rang out. The Porrellos were dead, their guard was fatally wounded and one of the assassins was hit. He would reappear in our family's story three decades later. I learned the Lonardos and Porrellos were the first two Italian-American Mafia families in Cleveland, part of a nationwide network that grew stronger during and after Prohibition.

Following the repeal of Prohibition, when booze was decriminalized, the next generation of mob leaders came to power. Many invested in gambling and nightclubs. Consequently, jazz and organized crime were often found under the same roof if at different tables. In his book *Dangerous Rhythms*, T.J. English wrote that Prohibition provided a framework for jazz.

"And it wasn't just that new venues created by the people's desire to imbibe were ready-made for jazz combos and dangerous rhythms. There was something about the Roaring Twenties itself—the clandestine social interactions, the pushing of racial boundaries, the hoodlums, the musicians—that turned jazz from a subculture into a telling representation of the national psyche..."

Mobsters infiltrated labor unions, using their power for profit. My father, a union officer, worked and socialized in nightclubs. With his surname resonating in underworld history, he befriended Cleveland's senior mob figures, including Frank Brancato. In 1932, Brancato survived a bullet to the stomach. A ballistics expert matched the bullet to a gun found at my grandfather's murder scene, but Brancato was never charged. He served time for perjury after lying about where he was shot.

I later learned that when my father was in his forties, he considered deepening his ties with the mob. One of them tested his loyalty by showing him a gruesome photo of his father's body. I suspected it was Brancato. My father already knew Brancato's role in the death. He ripped up the picture without a word. His message was clear:

"It was business. It's history."

Despite their shared past, they remained close—the son of a murdered man and one who likely pulled the trigger.

Though my dad was friendly with dangerous men, he heeded their advice to focus on his family. Had he gotten more involved, he might have ended up dead or in prison, like many others in Cleveland's underworld.

The mob scene was quiet in the 1960s but heated up in the early 1970s due to Danny Greene, an ambitious Irish-American racketeer. Greene, expelled from the longshoremen's union for embezzling, worked as an enforcer for Brancato and Shondor Birns while being an FBI informant. Birns, an aging mobster, farmed out muscle work to younger men and financed the city's illegal "numbers" racket, popular with both blacks and whites.

Brancato organized waste haulers into an association—members paid dues or risked damage to their property. Our neighbor, Big Mike Frato, got caught in this conflict. He'd built a successful disposal company from scratch, and his kids were like siblings to me. It was a time of innocence—until October 1971, when everything changed.

CHAPTER

4

My summer days included trips to the public pool, pickup base-ball games or biking around my neighborhood. I spent much of that time with my cousins, who lived in the other half of our duplex, and the Frato family, a few houses away. We darted in and out of back-yards, playing hide and seek or good-guy-bad-guy with toy guns.

At age nine, I was too young to know that Mike Frato was on a collision course with Danny Greene because of his refusal to pay membership dues to Brancato's rubbish guild.

Mr. Frato liked to gamble, and one of his regular spots was a card game in Coventry Village. This neighborhood of Cleveland Heights was alive with eclectic energy. Inside Record Revolution, music enthusiasts sifted through crowded shelves of vinyl. Outside the C-Saw Café, bikers gathered, their Harleys lined up in the street. The scent of Lebanese spices drifted from Tommy's Restaurant, where you could also enjoy a killer milkshake. My family often grabbed pies to go from Coventry Pizza. Above these shops was the apartment where Mike Frato played cards. One day, Danny Greene's enforcer found Frato's Cadillac parked nearby. He was planting a bomb when it detonated prematurely, killing him instantly. A month later Frato was killed in a shootout with Greene.

The shock lingered as Christmas approached. My father took me to shop for gifts for the Frato children, a quiet act of kindness that, over time, I would realize spoke volumes. It no doubt reminded him of the loss of his own father to violence—a tragedy he never spoke of.

Danny Greene eventually joined forces with John Nardi, a mob associate-turned-rival. They contributed to events and circumstances that hastened the decline of the American Mafia.

***

While I was still in elementary school, my class attended a special program at an arts center a half-hour drive from Cleveland Heights. I learned how to develop film in a darkroom and it sparked an interest in photography. After completing my homework and practicing my drum lesson, I also enjoyed tinkering with old electronic devices—taking old alarm clocks or radios apart, piece by piece. I learned a lesson: It's easier to take something apart than it is to reassemble it. It was a short-lived hobby. For television time, I graduated from *Superman* and *Batman* to *Adam-12* and *Police Woman*.

Around 1973, my father arranged for me to start drum lessons with Ray's first teacher, Ed Bobick. He came to our house and later taught out of a music store.

When Dad came home, his first question was inevitably, "Did you do your drum lesson?"

Soon he was prodding me to play for relatives like he'd done with my brother years earlier. By this time, Ray had joined the Cleveland Musicians Union. His studies continued and he started playing in nightclubs and lounges around the city. Ray practiced more than I did, often tapping away in the drum room, especially at night. During the day, Ray and I would turn up the volume and play along with our favorite bands, which included Buddy Rich, Count Basie,

Oscar Peterson, and Maynard Ferguson. Swing and bebop were our default, though we also enjoyed *Blood, Sweat & Tears*, *Earth, Wind & Fire*, and *Chicago*. Upstairs, the volume was muffled. My parents never complained, but playing in the evening was off-limits.

Taught informally by my brother and father, I quickly progressed with Ed Bobick, though I struggled with wanting to lead with my left hand or foot on a right-handed drum set. Ed guided me through numerous drum books.

While my brother was in the first years of his music career, I was at St. Ann's School, part of the parish where we attended church, grinding through seventh and eighth grade. Those two years would be my only parochial education, unlike my siblings, and probably due to the cost. However, I was required to attend classes in CCD, the Confraternity of Christian Doctrine.

By this time, it was just me and my mother attending church. Dad's presence was limited to baptisms, First Holy Communions, confirmations, weddings, and funerals. My brother and sister were now old enough to evade my mother's Sabbath day dragnet. As Mom and I made the five-minute drive to Saint Ann's, the bell tower came into view several blocks away. I often wondered how far I might see from the top. The church's gray stone edifice featured stately columns outside the grand entrance and throughout the vast museum-like interior.

I was taking drum lessons and playing along to jazz albums. My brother's new career was taking him on short tours with nationally known performers. One of Ray's most notable gigs was with Redd Foxx, the star of the television sitcom *Sanford and Son*. My father and I watched it often and shared many laughs. Redd Foxx had a raunchy stand-up comedy act and was coming to Cleveland's new Front Row Theater. He had a singer and another comedian on his show. Ray was hired for a six-piece band to accompany them on a two-week tour. The music director was trumpeter Harry "Sweets"

Edison from Columbus, Ohio. Sweets, an in-demand musician for concerts and recordings, was a Count Basie alumnus and a veteran of other big bands and small groups. My father was not shy about fostering friendships with performers who passed through town. He was a networker before the term became popular.

"You have to connect with people," he often told me and Ray.

When Maynard Ferguson, the Canadian trumpeter and band-leader, played Cleveland, my father invited him for dinner. It was the same with Sweets Edison, especially since he was friends with Louie Bellson. When Redd Foxx's Front Row gig kicked off, my father invited Sweets to our home after the show for a late meal and drink. But it wasn't to be.

My dad, Ray Porrello, Sr., with two jazz legends—drummer Gene Krupa, circa 1952, and vibraphonist Lionel Hampton, circa 1964.

In the drum room: my brother, Ray Porrello, Jr., at the drums with Louie Bellson and our father, Ray Porrello, Sr., circa 1970.

Me, age nine, with Louie Bellson.

My brother with comedian Redd Foxx, star of
Sanford and Son, in 1974.

Ray Porrello, Jr. with trumpeter Harry "Sweets" Edison in 1974.

Canadian trumpeter and bandleader Maynard
Ferguson, posing for my camera as he left our home.

CHAPTER 5

At 5:00 p.m. Ray had already left for the Redd Foxx show at the Front Row Theater. My sister was out. My mother had been cooking all day and made extra food in case Sweets brought anyone with him. But she prepared dinner for us at our usual time of 5:30. When Mom was ready, she called me and my father. My parents entertained guests at a polished table in our formal dining room. Daily family meals were in our eat-in kitchen at the four-seat table. It sat in a cramped corner between the gas stove and a window.

I squeezed past the window and a chair, then slid between the wall and table to sit in my usual spot. The electric coffee pot was on the table and plugged into a wall outlet between me and the stove. It had stopped percolating and sat steaming at the ready. The pot's chrome finish produced entrancing reflections from the room like a funhouse mirror. I was staring at it. Then I stood up.

I was never a klutz. I don't know why I stood up or lost my balance, but I fell on the cord, toppling the pot and dousing myself with that evil, blistering liquid. I screamed in pain and fright. My mother helped me up. As she pulled my steaming tee shirt over my head and off, a layer of skin from my chest came with it like paper-thin melted cheese. Mom was frantic as my father came running. They led me out the back door, down the porch steps and to the car.

My initial screams faded to moans as my mother blew on my chest to lessen the pain. While my father sped toward the hospital, Mom assured me that I would be okay. Meanwhile, my sister arrived home, stepped in the back door, and froze in shock. The table and chairs were askew, glasses overturned, and my tee shirt soaked with brown liquid on the floor. A crime scene? Susan called out for my mother and father. Silence. She knelt and prayed.

At the emergency room, the doctor stuck me with a syringe. Morphine. Instant, blessed relief. He and a nurse spent a half hour gently pulling away dead skin and applying gauze. The nurse wheeled me up to a hospital room. The morphine had relaxed me and I was getting comfortable. An hour later, my grandparents shuffled in.

My grandfather, thinking I looked well enough, chuckled. "Did you burn your scrotum?"

My grandmother shot him a look. I mustered a smile and assured him I had not.

"Ricky, what the hell happened?" my grandmother asked.

After I told her the story, she looked like she was going to cry. An hour later, my family members left, and I settled in for my first night in a hospital. My nurse was pleasant and upbeat.

Over the next two days, more family and friends came to visit me in the hospital. One of my father's business agents, a friendly black man with a perpetual smile, stopped in. One of my favorite teachers, a young nun, brought me balloons.

Treatment of the burned area was simple. Once daily, my nurse brushed on Betadine iodine solution to prevent infection. My pain gradually lessened. The initial swell of visitors dwindled and I got bored. My father brought in drumsticks and my practice pad, mounted on a tripod stand. One afternoon I was sitting on the side of my bed, tapping away. My favorite nurse came in and mentioned her love of music. She sat beside me and asked if I knew the song *Ol' Man River*. I said I did—a fast version from the U.S. Air Force *Airmen of Note* jazz band. She sang and I tapped along on my pad.

Sometimes, the nurses put me to work. I ran simple errands like delivering mail to the adjacent nursing station down the hall. They even let me sit at their desk to answer the intercom when a patient hit their call button.

"May I help you?" I would answer.

A nurse would take it from there. But when a patient complained about a child's voice answering, I lost my intercom gig.

After several days of the Betadine paint job, my nurse said, "You're eleven, you can do this yourself."

I faced the mirror and proudly performed the procedure myself. As the gauze dried, its corners lifted from my skin, and once a day, the doctor or nurse would gently pull and trim it away. Stretching exercises—like lifting my arm over my head—encouraged the elasticity of my skin. This routine continued for the remainder of the two weeks I was hospitalized.

It would take years for me to feel comfortable without a shirt, since the burns left permanent discoloration and scarring.

CHAPTER 6

On many evenings throughout the week, my father slipped into nightclubs, shaking hands with owners and bandleaders, and making sure union musicians got the gigs they deserved. He wasn't just enforcing rules—he loved the music and the musicians. As the head business agent for Local 4, my father's posts included the city's biggest venues. Backstage, he fostered business contacts and friendships with nationally known musicians. And through it all, he looked for opportunities to promote my brother.

Dad arranged for Louie Bellson's big band to perform a concert at the Bluegrass Motor Inn. The popular nightclub's clientele included Cleveland mob members and their associates. My father hosted a big table with our immediate family, some cousins, and close friends to hear Louie and watch Ray take over the drum chair for two songs. In the world of jazz music, veterans traditionally invite promising young players to "sit in" with their bands. It was my first time in a nightclub and the experience was sensory overload: a haze of cigarette smoke, and the powerful band, mere feet from our table. When Ray performed, Louie stood off to the side, smiling in approval. I observed the scene intently, noticing the expressions of the soloists and catching every familiar move my brother made, all while my heart beat rapidly as if it were me playing the drums.

Another time, my father arranged for Louie to conduct a drum clinic—an educational presentation and performance—at the musicians' union. Local 4 members, mostly hip drummers in full-length leather coats and stylish caps, packed the room. Louie started his presentation with one of his signature five-minute solos. He could compose a percussive symphony and extract atypical sounds from barely audible grace notes on the cymbal bells to precisely executed and thunderous rolls on the snare drum and bass drums. At his final cymbal crash, Louie let the applause settle before making his point—solos were fine, but a drummer's true job was to keep time and keep the band propelled and swinging.

Louie's passion for educating young drummers was evident. Once again, he invited my brother to sit in on a second drum kit for a short performance and a drum "battle." Afterward, Louie spoke of the importance of commitment to learning. He was always open to new ideas, even from students. Louie conducted dozens of clinics each year. He valued the passing of the jazz drumming tradition across generations:

"Someone showed my mentors, my mentors showed me, and now I show the next generation," he said.

After the clinic and at my father's request, Cleveland's mayor presented Louie with the key to the city. My father had hired a photographer, and Louie graciously posed with many of the drummers. He even called me over for a shot where he and my brother pretended to break my arms.

That afternoon, one thing stood out to me. It was Louie's love of drumming and playing with musicians, shown by his ever-present smile. I seldom witnessed that with other musicians on stage. But it wasn't just performing that lit him up. He enjoyed people.

Someone once said, "Louie Bellson never says anything bad

about anyone."

He was a shining example of the camaraderie musicians have for each other. Jazz players in particular are part of a great American tradition that crosses generations and social and racial boundaries. Pearl Bailey, Louie's first wife, wrote about the love between musicians and their greetings with hugs. She called it "mutual adoration."

Louie Bellson and trumpeter Clark Terry had mutual adoration. Recognized for his distinctive style, Terry popularized the use of the flugelhorn in jazz. He was also known for his amusing scat tune, *Mumbles*. Louie and Clark affectionately called each other "Scunge," short for *scungilli*, an Italian snail delicacy.

Louie explained to me the meaning: "I would crawl for you."

Trombonist Nick DiMaio, Louie's band manager and friend, was a sweetheart of a man. Often Louie's regular band traveled with him, but if he used local players, Nick's job was to rehearse the band a day early.

Though Louie was serious about the quality of his musicians, he had a sense of humor that shone through his personality. In the 1970s, Nick DiMaio was not in the best health. While he and Louie were golfing, Nick had a heart attack. He survived and eventually went back to work. Louie later joked about being on a golf course when it happened:

"I had to hit the ball—then drag Nick. Hit the ball—drag Nick."

There was nothing funny in the final chapter of another Bellson trombonist—Frank Rosolino, whose solos were instantly recognizable. He could hit high notes with clarity and blow with the fluency of a trumpeter. He was a cut-up who cracked four jokes a minute, but his success and whimsical personality belied a dark psyche. Following his wife's suicide, he spoke to friends about the struggles he and his two young sons faced. Not long after, Rosolino shocked loved ones and the jazz world after shooting both sons, killing one, and then taking his own life. The surviving boy was permanently blinded. I enjoy Frank Rosolino's recordings and still marvel at his skill. Still, I find it difficult at times to separate talent from tragedy.

***

In late 1974, Count Basie was searching for a new drummer. My brother had no idea that a career-changing phone call was coming when Louie Bellson recommended him, leading to an audition and a new gig. My family celebrated, but Ray's gig with the eminent swing band was ill-fated.

Meanwhile, at eleven years old, I practiced drums for thirty to ninety minutes daily, and continued playing along to jazz albums. It didn't feel like practice—I enjoyed it.

Almost daily my father reinforced my education. "Did you do your drum lesson?"

With a father and older brother who were drummers, music seemed like my destiny—until one Christmas morning when a gift changed everything.

CHAPTER
7

On weeknights, when I was finally old enough to stay up until 11:30, I'd join my parents to watch the beloved king of late-night television crack jokes. NBC's *The Tonight Show, starring Johnny Carson*, opened with a 10-minute monologue that pulled laughs from the headlines. Then came the guests—singers, comedians, and actors who performed or chatted with Johnny and his jolly sidekick, Ed McMahon. Sometimes zookeepers brought wild animals on stage.

Half the thrill for me was the band, arguably the most famous group in television history. But my connection ran deeper than admiration. Many of Louie Bellson's musicians also played for the Tonight Show band. And on the nights when Louie filled in for regular drummer Ed Shaughnessy, it felt like magic—having a little piece of my own world on that stage.

***

My brother had been with the Count Basie Orchestra for about six weeks. They were playing Chicago when Ray was visited by a Cleveland friend. After the concert, they decided to go see a band.

They got in the car. There was a crash. Ray was injured. He came home to recover but soon felt worse. A doctor discovered Ray was bleeding to death from a ruptured spleen. He was rushed to surgery. Meanwhile, Count Basie brought in Butch Miles, a peppy stickman in the style of Buddy Rich, to fill in for Ray.

Weeks after Ray's accident, Basie came to Cleveland. My father invited the band for dinner. My parents served two dozen musicians and friends at tables stretching from the kitchen through the dining room and into the living room. Armed with my camera, I prowled for good shots. There were pleasant smiles from saxophonists Bobby Plater and John Williams. The Count himself shot me a playful scowl as I snapped his picture mid-bite.

I was having fun until my father turned to me: "Why don't you play a tune for the guys?"

It wasn't a suggestion, and Dad reached for our camera.

Performing for adult guests at home was my first experience with stage jitters—my heart rate went into overdrive, and my face flushed beet red. Reluctantly, I headed to the basement. Several band members followed. A few others stopped short and sat on the steps. I set the needle on a big band track, cranked the volume, and played along. At my final cymbal crash, they applauded. A few musicians posed with me as my father snapped pictures. At age eleven, it felt like more of a moment for Dad than for me.

By the time Ray recovered, Butch Miles had solidified his place in the band. It was a tough break for Ray, but losing the gig led him to something bigger—something that later would change my own path.

***

The gift was a *Patrolman 6*, a multi-band radio from Radio Shack, my favorite store. Though other broadcasts, like airline pilots or taxicab dispatchers, were intriguing, none caught my attention like the police. After a few days, my parents became interested as well. The radio was kept on a table in the living room. We developed an ear for the excited chatter of serious calls—a traffic accident with injuries or a robbery—and would turn the volume up. During subsequent years, while much of my family's delight centered on my brother's music career, I had one ear on that radio, listening and dreaming.

CHAPTER 8

When my brother lost his gig with Count Basie after a car accident, Louie Bellson recommended him to George Rhodes, Sammy Davis Jr.'s conductor. Louie had recently filled in as Sammy's drummer for a few weeks, and he put in a word for Ray. My brother aced his audition and got the job.

When my mother told me the news, she was thrilled. She wanted me to guess who Ray's new boss was.

"He has a television show, and he's black."

I thought for a moment. "I don't know, Ma."

"He sings and dances."

I shrugged, clueless.

"He does impressions."

"I don't know, Ma."

"Sammy Davis!"

Sammy Davis?

"Yes," my mother squealed. "Sammy Davis, Jr!"

At age thirteen, I knew Sammy Davis, Jr. was famous, but only later, after reading his autobiographies, did I grasp how his life and career had intertwined with history. Sammy was born in 1925 to

Sam Davis, Sr., a member of Will Mastin's tap dance act, and Elvera Sanchez, a dancer. He was three when his parents divorced, and his father took him on the road. Will Mastin's show was well-known on the national Vaudeville circuit of variety-entertainment theaters. Sammy affectionately referred to Mastin as his uncle. He had minimal contact with his traveling mother, so his paternal grandmother lovingly filled the void.

Sammy started mimicking Mastin's silly faces, prompting the elders to bring him on stage. The toddler soon dazzled audiences with his boundless energy as a dancer. By the time Sammy was five, Mastin had renamed his group *Will Mastin and Gang, featuring Little Sammy Davis, Jr.* Critics dubbed the boy "the greatest juvenile entertainer in the world."

Sammy had no formal schooling; his father and uncle taught him entertainment. They stressed dressing well and giving his all. As Sammy matured, he craved more knowledge. He watched acts from the wings, analyzing and gauging reactions. In his downtime, he watched movies, studied actors' voices, listened to records, and taught himself to play the drums.

As Vaudeville declined, the song and dance trio soldiered on, moving from city to city. Meanwhile, young Sammy grappled with bigotry and segregation. The group celebrated pay increases and weathered lean times. When the elders couldn't afford meals, they made sure Sammy ate. As the slightly built boy hit his teens, his agility, energy, and ambition elevated the act. Sammy became the trio's star.

In 1941, sixteen-year-old Sammy and his father tried to enlist after Japan attacked Pearl Harbor. Sammy was too young; his father was too old. By that time, Vaudeville was a bygone era. On the nightclub circuit, Sammy looked for ways to refine his talent. He was annoyed by fellow black performers who relied on clichés, spoke in "colored" vernacular, and failed to connect. Conversely, he was impressed by entertainers like Frank Sinatra, who developed a rapport with their audiences, even "touching their emotions."

Sammy perfected his impressions of actors and singers, many of them white. Audiences loved them. Sammy's vision, passion, and dynamism propelled the Will Mastin Trio's popularity. But in 1944, Sammy was drafted into the army. In basic training, racism exploded as fellow soldiers attacked him verbally and physically over his skin color. At five-foot-five and 125 pounds, Sammy fought back ferociously. Sergeant Williams, an avid reader, took an interest in counseling him. He encouraged Sammy to read from his classic literature collection.

"Sergeant Williams was my savior," Sammy said years later. "He taught me to read and write."

When Williams learned about Sammy's background, he recommended him for shows. Sammy was warmly received, even by his attackers. He reveled in the power of his talent. Impressed commanders transferred him to the Special Services Unit, where he performed in military camps across the U.S. In 1945, Sammy was honorably discharged and rejoined his dad and uncle. At the time, Frank Sinatra, a decade older than Sammy, was well on his way to superstardom and usually featured a black act. In 1947, Sinatra insisted the Will Mastin Trio be hired to open his Capitol Theater show. It marked the start of a lifelong friendship between Frank and Sammy.

"Frank took me under his wing," Sammy would later recall.

In 1951, the trio shined at Ciro's, a Hollywood hotspot for celebrities and mobsters. The show opened doors for Sammy and sparked friendships with a circle of Hollywood's Golden Age stars led by Humphrey Bogart. Bogart frequently hosted a lively group of fellow entertainers, including Sinatra. Bogey's wife, Lauren Bacall, jokingly referred to her husband's inner circle as a "rat pack."

Sammy embraced his growing network while honing his craft.

When Bogart died in 1957, Frank Sinatra continued hobnobbing with his closest buddies, Sammy Davis, Jr. and Dean Martin. The trio formed the core members of the better-known *Rat Pack*. Their music was hip and swingin'. And so were they.

Sammy's talent and passion transcended racial discrimination. His efforts raised the Mastin group's fee and helped break down color barriers. Despite enduring Jim Crow laws and cruel racist assaults, he disapproved of discrimination in any form. When Sammy proposed Morton (Morty) Stevens, a white clarinetist and arranger, to serve as conductor, Will Mastin opposed the choice. He said their show was a colored act.

Sammy shot back, "It's not a colored act... It's just a plain act."

Sammy stood firm. Mastin relented and they hired Stevens. Morty remained as conductor until their pianist, George Rhodes, took over in 1958.

In *Gonna Do Great Things*, biographer Gary Fishgall observed that Sammy's assessment of someone's traits or talent rejected race. He sought the finest friends and employees. Their skin color just didn't matter.

In the 1950s, Sammy expanded his career by recording albums, performing on Broadway, and acting in movies. In 1954, while playing Vegas, he agreed to record the title track to a film. The decision to squeeze in a quick road trip to a Los Angeles studio would be life-altering. An assistant accompanied him for the four-hour drive. Three hours into the trip, Sammy neared a curve in San Bernardino. Up ahead, an elderly woman missed her turn. She stopped to back up. The force of the collision slammed Sammy's face into the center cone of the steering wheel, breaking facial bones and severely damaging his left eye. His assistant and the occupants of the other car suffered serious but non-life-threatening injuries. Sammy was rushed to a hospital, where a specialist eventually performed surgery and removed his eye.

As he lay in his bed, the twenty-nine-year-old entertainer had many spiritual questions about his life for the hospital chaplain, who was a rabbi. How did he survive such a severe accident? How had he risen to such success? The rabbi suggested he look inward for the answers. Only two months later, Sammy returned to the stage, more popular than ever. He wore a patch before getting a prosthetic eye. Over the next few years, Sammy studied Jewish history. Some friends supported his desire to convert. Others saw it as a publicity stunt. Sammy believed Blacks and Jews shared a history of oppression.

"He admired the Jewish people's history of overcoming adversity," wrote historian Rebecca L. Davis. "Where others saw impossibility, [Sammy] claimed logical compatibility."

Judaism provided the spiritual strength he needed. In 1960, Sammy formally converted.

***

In 1959, Sammy celebrated thirty years in show business. Reporters called him the "king of the nightclubs" and "Mr. Entertainment." Sam Sr. and Will Mastin retired in the 1960s, and Sammy's solo career soared. By then he was a multi-talented phenomenon widely known as "the greatest entertainer in the world."

He was SAMMY.

But black patrons were still barred from Las Vegas showrooms. Sammy knew that his ability to draw crowds was a weapon against racism. At the Copa Room of the Sands Hotel and Casino, he refused to perform until his grandmother and other family members had a front-row table. He helped to desegregate Las Vegas, successfully challenging the Sands president to hire black employees.

Despite fearing violence, Sammy marched in civil rights rallies led by Dr. Martin Luther King and Reverend Jesse Jackson while donating time and money to causes benefiting blacks and children.

Despite his generosity, Sammy was denounced whenever his actions conflicted with the expectations of blacks, whites, and the media. Entertaining white audiences, supporting Republican Richard Nixon, and converting to Judaism seemed to bring out criticism at every juncture.

When Sammy met with militant activists, one of them harshly disparaged his immersion in white America:

"You is black. But you don't be black."

Sammy's romances with white women sparked more than criticism. The threats got worse when he married Swedish actress May Britt. At the time, mixed marriages were illegal in most states. Amid bomb threats and hate letters, Sammy hired bodyguards and off-duty cops. Eventually he started carrying a gun.

Despite Sammy's struggles with hatred and discrimination, his experiences were marked by profound irony. In his autobiography, *Yes I Can*, Sammy wrote that when he faced racism, it was most often a white person who stepped in to help him.

Sammy struggled to balance his success and personal freedom with criticism—some called his views misguided, others felt his contributions weren't enough. But he remained unabashed and unwavering in his philosophy of relationships. When he received a humanitarian award from the NAACP in 1971, he explained that he judged people by their honesty and dignity.

At Sammy's Beverly Hills home, a plaque greeted visitors:

"This house welcomes all colors, races, and religions as long as they have peace and love in their hearts."

CHAPTER

9

When my brother joined Sammy Davis, Jr.'s band, the Cleveland newspapers took notice. It was a proud moment for our family. Musicians called Dad or sent notes of congratulations. He eagerly made solo trips to Las Vegas to see Ray. My father reveled in backstage life, greeting Sammy, chatting with the band and buying conductor George Rhodes a drink.

The TV show *Sammy and Company* showcased Sammy with an all-star big band and a variety of celebrities. Repeat guests included comedians Richard Pryor, Tom Dreesen, Redd Foxx, and singers Steve Lawrence and Sarah Vaughan. The show was the highlight of our evenings, especially when Ray appeared on screen.

In October 1975, Sammy returned to Cleveland's Front Row where, fifteen months earlier, he had opened the theater-in-the-round. My father got tickets. It would be our family's first time seeing Ray perform live with Sammy.

I packed my Instamatic camera. But before the show, an announcement banned audience photos. Luckily, Sammy, an avid photographer, took mercy. During his show, he suspended the rule for a minute and invited anyone wanting a photograph of him to fire away. The crowd erupted in applause. Appreciative chatter continued as flashes lit the house. I snapped a picture. My father encouraged me to get out of my seat for a closer shot. I hesitated. He prodded and nudged me into the aisle. The flashes had slowed, and Sammy was ready to continue his show, but he spotted me approaching. He moved close to three steps leading to the stage. I stepped up, aiming my camera.

He smiled warmly, bent down, and greeted me, "Hey, little man."

I snapped a photo, smiled, and turned around as the audience applauded Sammy's charming gesture with the kid photographer.

As Sammy sang, danced, and joked, my attention shifted between him, George Rhodes, and my brother. The band was in the orchestra pit, and I got good views of Ray and the other musicians. My brother played with both command and finesse. The rhythm section was tight, and Al McKibbon's bold bass sound provided a solid foundation for the music. I watched as Ray and the band followed George Rhodes' arm and hand directions with precision. The licks and fills that Ray played to set up powerful band entrances were familiar to me from hearing him practice with albums in the drum room.

***

In 1976, I juggled junior high school, my homework, and drum lessons. In my music studies, I advanced to polyrhythms and big band drum chart interpretation. Drum set parts are seldom written note for note—there's just too much going on. A drummer must interpret music more than any other jazz musician. One of my teacher's most valuable assignments was to have me transcribe drum parts from jazz recordings.

The exercise emphasized what Ed Bobick stressed: being a good listener.

"Have big ears," he'd say.

Being a good listener was also one of Louie Bellson's core principles. It was advice I took seriously.

My father also got me started on the piano with a teacher who came to the house. It was good timing because I wanted to express myself musically beyond just percussion and air saxophone.

***

I spent some of my free time riding my bike through the neighborhood with cousins and friends. One summer afternoon, I was in the high school parking lot across from my house. I heard a firecracker pop off in the distance. Two minutes later, my mother's voice sliced through the air. She sounded alarmed. I pedaled back across the street. As I neared, she shouted, "Get in the house!"

Inside, the police radio was buzzing with activity. Someone robbed the gas station on the other side of the school. The owner's German Shepherd had been shot dead. I sat next to the radio in sadness for the dog. The robbers escaped. "Don't let the owner take the dog," a supervisor ordered. "We're gonna need the slug for evidence."

Hearing the police responding to emergencies sparked an interest in law enforcement. When a cousin joined the force, I attended his police academy graduation as part of my junior high school civics class project. And through my father's friend, a police captain, I got a tour of the station house. I took photographs for my presentation and developed them in my dark room. When my cousin got comfortable in his job, he would stop at our house occasionally, especially on holidays when he was not busy. On other days, when the police officers started arriving at the high school for the football games, I'd ride over on my bike and strike up a conversation.

Meanwhile, underworld violence escalated and local bombings captured newspaper headlines. I was in our sunroom when the desk phone rang. Mom answered. It was my father, and he was going to be late. John Nardi, a labor union official and Cleveland Mafia associate, had just been murdered with a car bomb across from Dad's office. A few months later, racketeer Danny Greene was killed the same way.

***

Now and then Sammy gave members of his entourage gifts like a boom box cassette tape player with a tiny built-in television and a silk tour jacket from his Broadway show *Stop the World–I Want to Get Off.* When Ray had time off, he often brought home photographs and mementos. He had been to Japan recently and got a personalized photo of drummer and bandleader George Kawaguchi, who worked with the *Sharps and Flats* jazz orchestra.

My family looked forward to Sammy's appearances on television, hoping for a glimpse of Ray. One of the best opportunities came in 1977 when Sammy subbed for Johnny Carson for three nights. He featured the Tonight Show band led by George Rhodes. The up-tempo tune had solo space for several musicians, including my brother. It was a proud moment to see him on TV and hear, "On drums: Ray Porrello." Later, as I lay in bed, the world around me would fade, and I'd drift off, imagining myself behind those same drums, playing for Sammy.

CHAPTER 10

By 1977, I'd been learning drums for eight years, with three spent in private lessons. I'd advanced beyond the basics and was now learning fine points, developing my solo abilities, and playing to records on the drum set daily. My father and brother often coached me. I was learning colorful jargon as we listened to our favorite artists. It was an ultimate peer compliment for a jazz musician to be described as a "bitchin" player or one who performed so impressively, who swung so hard, that certain below-the-waist body parts, as the saying went, detached. For example:

"That guy plays his *ass* off!"

There were... even more colorful variations.

I had been studying the piano for a year. My teacher added easy jazz tunes to my weekly lessons. I also studied music theory in high school. I had no affinity for school except for the music program. I was a "B" student but struggled with math. I still tried my best. The music department was the center of my high school years. The emphasis was on concert bands and symphony orchestras, but the directors also offered a jazz ensemble. Percussionists had to march to perform with this group. I didn't want to march, but I gave in to play jazz. Eventually, I was appointed as the marching band's co-head percussionist. My partner and I rehearsed the drum squad and created cadences to synchronize the band's movements.

The jazz ensemble had many excellent players. They'd sometimes come over to practice big band music in the drum room. I would pull a chart from my brother's big band book and play the song on the record player. The high school band's repertoire included Maynard Ferguson and Chick Corea arrangements. Sometimes, the director let me bring in a Louie Bellson or Count Basie chart for us to play.

That group and the concept of a jazz big band always brought me great enjoyment in listening and practicing. However, performing with the Cleveland Heights High School jazz ensemble made the experience feel tangible and made me appreciate how each musician interpreted the sheet music—those small black dots and lines organized on white paper—within the rules of music, all driven by a certain rhythm or groove. There was a sense of belonging and teamwork—individuals combined into sections—the saxophones, the trombones, the trumpets. A pianist, a guitarist, a bassist, a drummer, and a vibraphonist comprised the rhythm section. And all of us, led by the conductor, worked toward a common goal. The feelings of accomplishment—elation even—came not just at a final note, the end of a rehearsal, or the end of a performance. They came within and throughout the tunes—moments of spirited inspiration during individual or section solos and shout choruses—the spirited climax of a big band arrangement. We even recorded our own album. Our school year efforts concluded with a "Jazz Night" concert.

***

I should have been excited. My father told me Louie Bellson was sponsoring a national drum contest. Thirty-seven years earlier, Louie was seventeen years old when he won the Gene Krupa drum competition. Motivated by a passion for teaching young musicians, he wanted to reprise the event. He approached officials at the Slingerland Drum Company. They formed the Slingerland and Louie Bellson National Drum Contest. My father picked up a copy of *Modern Drummer* magazine. The announcement and registration form were in it. The contest was split into local, regional, semi-final, and final competitions. I feared disappointing my father, but I also worried about ending up on stage at the finals in Las Vegas. Encouraged by my father and brother, I filled out the entry form and sent it in with a twenty-five dollar registration fee provided by my father.

***

At sixteen, I was finally old enough to join the musicians union. My father drove me to Local 4. When we got inside, he insisted, with a subtle grin, that regardless of your primary instrument, an audition on the piano was mandatory. Half a dozen ladies from the office staff went along with him egging me on. As they stood smiling, I sat down at the lobby piano and played an Antonio Carlos Jobim bossa nova called *Meditation*. I set up a big ending and deliberately ended on a wrong note, getting the laugh I hoped for. I left with my Local 4 membership card. When I returned home, my father gave me a new, smaller drum kit—perfect for the local gigs I hoped to soon play.

In the weeks that followed, my father referred me to a local trumpeter who used to work in Las Vegas. He took me on as his drummer. Dad wanted to drive me to my first gig, a wedding reception.

"You're just going to drop me off, right, Dad?" I asked.

"Yeah, and I'll pick you up after."

I loaded my new drums into his car early, then took a shower. I dried off while looking in the mirror at my chest, trying to convince myself that after five years, the burn scars no longer bothered me. I put on my suit, which was navy blue, and borrowed one of my father's many ties. Dad always dressed well—suits for work. Even when running errands, he looked good. I had some hand-me-down clothes from my brother. And my hair had gone from wavy to curly, so I started using a pick like him.

There were two prevailing styles for young men in my neighborhood: collegiate and rack. Collegiate was a softer look—perhaps a sweater over a dress shirt with a button-down collar, corduroy trousers, and loafers. "Rack," for racketeer, was a slicker style reminiscent of jazz musicians and the 1950s-1960s gangster look. We were definitely rack.

Dad drove me to the party center. He helped me carry my drums to the stage. The other members of the quartet knew him and welcomed us warmly. I hoped Dad would leave, but instead, he started helping me unpack. It felt awkward—I wanted to prove I could handle it on my own without him worrying about me.

"Dad, it's okay. I got it."

"Alright," he said. "I'll see you later."

As he walked away, I felt a surge of independence and confidence.

It was just a four-piece group—trumpet, bass guitar, drums, and Cordovox—an electric accordion. The music flowed easily—medium swing tunes, bossa novas, polkas, ballads, and a couple of light rock numbers. For the first few tunes, the other musicians shot me smiles and nods. The bandleader was casual. He counted some songs off, but now and then he just started playing, and the rest of us quickly joined in. During a break, we even got to eat, though we had to make it quick.

For my second gig, Dad let me borrow his car and go myself. Before I left, though, he quizzed me.

"Do you know where it is?"

"I have directions, Dad."

"They have more than one room at that party center, so make

sure you unload at the right one. And make sure you leave the house early. I don't want you rushing."

"I will."

If Mom and Dad were awake when I got home, more questions followed.

"How did it go?"

"Good, Dad."

My mother would chime in from another room. "Did they feed you?"

"No, Ma, not this time."

"Okay, there's lunch meat. Go make a sandwich."

By my third or fourth gig, my parents seemed more at ease with me driving myself, confident I could handle the job. But if anyone still had worries, it was my mother.

Meanwhile, the Slingerland and Louie Bellson National Drum Contest got underway. The local competition was at DAL Drum Studio in Erie, Pennsylvania, two hours from Cleveland. My father's cousin, Jim, tagged along.

When we entered the drum shop, about thirty people were milling about. Folding chairs filled only half the space. That was okay because I didn't feel like sitting. The owner, the contest host, welcomed us. As we were milling around, a man recognized my father. He was a drummer from Cleveland serving as one of the judges. They greeted each other and chatted briefly about the music business.

I mingled with other contestants, twelve of us ranging from thirteen to eighteen. The contest involved sight reading, playing along to small group and big band recordings, and performing a three-minute solo. I was one of the last to perform in the back room, where only the contestants and judges were present. After the last player, the judges spent thirty minutes tabulating their scores. Meanwhile, the contestants chatted quietly with their family members. I was standing with my dad and cousin near a corner when the host called for attention. "Ladies and gentlemen, I'm pleased to announce the winner of this local competition of the Louie Bellson and Slingerland Drum Company national drum contest. The winner is Rick Porrello."

I couldn't believe it. I won! My father and cousin were beaming. They shook my hand, and I walked over to the host. He awarded me the winner's plaque and a contest tee shirt. I thanked him. Everyone was applauding while a shop employee snapped a Polaroid photo. I glanced at the crowd. Everyone was smiling except one woman sitting in the middle of the room. She wasn't clapping.

Several people near me offered handshakes and words of congratulations. Once more, I noticed the woman. Her face was red, and she was staring down and off to the side. Suddenly, she arose and headed for the shop owner. I heard every word. She was upset that the one judge knew my father. It was an obvious insinuation that some injustice had taken place against her son. As the crowd looked on, mouths agape, the contest host reasoned diplomatically with the woman. He explained that my father was a musicians' union official and the judges were musicians. It was not surprising that they would be acquainted. The joy of the moment drained away. Some of the parents rolled their eyes and shook their heads.

Across the room I saw my father's jaw clenched as his steel-blue eyes bore holes through the woman. Fortunately, he and my cousin kept their cool and let the shop owner handle the woman. Her husband stood silently in the background, avoiding her rant. She finally stopped to breathe, and the shop owner disappeared into the back room. A minute later, the judges came out, took the woman aside, and spoke with her. The judge in question admitted that he knew my father from the music business. He and the other judges assured her that they scored each of the contestants honestly and only according to their performances.

The woman calmed down but still fumed. It seemed that she was certain that her son would win. When the shop owner announced my name, her hopes were shattered. I thought her complaint had ended, but she was desperate. She walked over to me. My father loomed near as she spoke.

"If the officials will allow, would you mind if my son joined you in the regional competition?"

I shrugged. "No, I don't mind." I figured if I beat him once, I could do it again.

My father, cousin, and I forced smiles as the shop owner snapped two more Polaroids and congratulated me again. He quietly apologized to us for the scene the woman made and wished me good luck in the regionals.

My father turned to me. "Let's get the hell out of here."

***

The regional competition was held in September 1979 at Capital University in Columbus, Ohio. About twenty kids from the Midwest competed for a spot in the semi-finals. The woman's son wasn't among them. I later learned officials denied her request.

The heat was on, but I left Columbus as the winner and earned a spot among thirteen regional winners who would get all travel expenses paid for themselves, their parents, and their drum teacher to participate in the semi-finals and finals in Las Vegas. I thought I might actually win this. I was nervous, unsure if I even wanted to. I loved to play drums, but one of the prizes for the first place finalist was an appearance with Louie Bellson on Johnny Carson's Tonight Show. That possibility made my heart race. But my family's excitement was contagious and I decided to go for it. Making it to the finals meant performing with Louie's band—a prize in itself.

A few days later, a letter from Capital University's percussion director pumped me up even more. He congratulated me on my performance and said he was looking forward to seeing me on the Johnny Carson show.

Meanwhile, Sammy returned to the Front Row Theater, where my family attended the show. Afterward, Ray brought us backstage. Sammy wore a big smile as he shook our hands. Dad had already met him at some of Ray's earlier gigs. Sammy posed for a photograph with my family and we hung out in his dressing room for fifteen minutes. He was relaxed, sitting on the sofa with his shoes off and legs up and joking with friends.

***

Each of the thirteen semi-final contestants would compete on a drum set arranged to their specifications courtesy of the Slingerland Drum Company. I made a list of what I wanted—Louie Bellson's most recent twin bass drum setup—and mailed it. In the coming days, I spent much of my time in the drum room practicing and wondering what Las Vegas would be like.

In my early teens, I often heard stories of relatives' trips to Las Vegas—big-name shows, low-cost buffets, and the allure of the casinos. They told of playing blackjack, roulette, craps, and the slot machines. It seemed they always "almost won"—at least that's how they made it sound. But they always had fun:

"I only lost sixty bucks, but I saw two incredible shows and the buffets were cheap and really good."

Some of them traded the bitter Cleveland winters for the dry, blazing heat of the desert sun. Many got jobs at casinos. Clevelanders heading west often received advice to apply first at the Desert Inn Hotel and Casino. Years later I would learn why.

My mother did not want to go on the trip. Getting time off from her job as a sales clerk at May Company, flying, and the stress of her youngest child competing in a national contest would be too much for her. So my sister Susan took her place. On the other hand, my father was enthusiastic and no doubt eager to see how my participation might shape my future.

Arriving in Las Vegas, I was astounded to see people playing slot machines right at the airport. On a moving walkway toward the exit, the recorded voices of celebrities played over a loudspeaker:

"Welcome to Las Vegas. Please stand to the right and pass on the left."

The Ambassador Inn was a few blocks from the famous Las Vegas Boulevard area known as "the Strip." It was the official hotel for contestants. The contest administrators stayed there, too. One of them had a pretty daughter about my age. I wanted to say hello to her but never mustered the courage, even after passing her several times. The officials held a meeting for the contestants and their families.

Afterward my father rented a car. The golden Nevada sun was setting when we went to dinner and then checked out downtown. I snapped photos of Fremont Street lit up with thousands of bulbs on the Four Queens, Golden Nugget, and other casinos. On the Strip, it was the same—the brilliant lighting mimicking daylight.

I continued snapping away—the Sands, the Flamingo. Then came the most impressive of all: Caesars Palace. The opulence of this Vegas icon started at the street, where a columned marquee currently heralded TOM JONES. There was a long reflecting pool with high-streaming fountains flanked by rows of tall trees that led past Roman statues to the grand entrance. I couldn't help but chuckle at the bare-breasted goddess, water shooting from her nipples. I would learn that the resort's name—Caesars Palace—had no apostrophe. The plural form suggested that everyone who entered would be treated like an emperor or empress.

The night before the contest, my father took us to see an all-star jazz combo featuring Jack Sheldon. He led the Merv Griffin TV show band and was appearing at a small club called the Hofbrau

Haus. Before the night was over, my father encouraged me to introduce myself to drummer Nick Ceroli. Originally from Youngstown,
Ohio, he subbed for Ed Shaughnessy on The Tonight Show. We
talked briefly and he wished me good luck.

**

The semi-finals and finals took place at the University of Nevada
Las Vegas and were judged by well-known music professors and
performers. I recognized the names Peter Erskine from the band
Weather Report and, of course, Doc Severinsen. Reporters from several newspapers and Modern Drummer Magazine covered the event.

The requirements for the semi-finals were similar to those for
the local and regional competitions: sight reading, playing along
with jazz recordings, and performing an extended solo. The thirteen
contestants had twenty minutes to practice in private. I remembered
my dad's advice: *Just play like you do in the basement.* I sweated heav-
ily before and during my performance.

Afterward my thoughts raced. My father, sister and drum teacher
waited nervously. Would I make the finals or head home with only
a semi-finalist plaque? When my name was called as one of the four
finalists, I was momentarily embarrassed by my sister's scream. My
father smiled. I couldn't believe I might win. We shook hands with
strangers before heading to the Ambassador Inn for dinner. How
could I eat? I was about to perform with the Louie Bellson band.

The final competition was held in the university auditorium,
which seated about fifteen hundred. The event was set up like a
show, with Wayne Newton who was known as Las Vegas's "Midnight
Idol" as the emcee. A large banner behind the drum riser read:
SLINGERLAND DRUM COMPANY – LOUIE BELLSON
NATIONAL DRUM CONTEST – FINALS. Louie's band was in
place, joined by father and son conga players in front of the drums.

The evening started with an introduction by the host, the

university's band director, and then comments by the president of Slingerland. Louie performed with his band. Then Wayne Newton, a former semi-professional drummer, came out to show Louie a few things. He manned a Slingerland set identical to Louie's except for the bass drum heads, which read "WN." Louie played the straight man. Wayne's attempts to keep up in the mock drum battle drew laughs. Finally, he reached behind his drums and produced a pair of drumsticks—three feet long—that brought more laughter. That capped the routine. Afterward, Wayne and the contest officials gave brief speeches.

The final competition had the four finalists performing one song with an extended solo. I spotted familiar faces in Louie's band, including bassist John Heard and trumpeter Bobby Shew. I'd met others when they played in Cleveland, and my father invited them over for dinner. Despite my stage jitters, I felt happy and privileged to perform with these great musicians. And that was a good thing. I took fourth place but was thankful to be among the finalists— and even more thankful the contest was over. Hank Guaglianone, from Rolling Meadows, Illinois, won first place. The four finalists received tom-tom trophies, the largest for the winner and the smallest for fourth place. As the crowd left, some came to the stage to compliment our performances. A woman in dark glasses and a bulky overcoat waved me over. I bent down, and to my surprise, it was Pearl Bailey, Louie Bellson's wife.

"You were quite the professional with Louie's band," she said matter-of-factly.

"Thank you, Ms. Bailey."

Contest officials ushered us backstage, and we mingled with our families, the judges, Louie Bellson and Wayne Newton. Doc Severinsen approached me. He said he had voted for me for first place. "You're the kind of player I'd hire for the Tonight Show," he said. I was taken aback at his compliment and almost jokingly asked if Ed Shaughnessy was leaving soon. Instead, I thanked him and stood by my father. Slingerland officials arranged photos with Louie and Wayne Newton. Along with my trophy and the stressful Vegas trip, I received a check for one thousand dollars.

When I got settled back home, I reviewed the contest score sheets and the judges' comments. Two of them suggested I focus more on dynamics—the shifts in volume and intensity during a song or solo. Louie Bellson also provided feedback:

"Great with the band. Just keep playing."

My mother, Betty, with Count Basie after he and his
band had dinner at our house in 1975.

Basie alto saxophonist Bobby Plater.

Me, age eleven, after playing along to a tune for the
Count Basie band in our basement. Guitarist Freddie
Green and drummer Butch Miles lean in for my
father's camera.

Sammy Davis, Jr. greets me—"Hey, little man"—as I approach
the stage to take his picture at Cleveland's Front Row Theater,
circa 1974.

Sammy and some of his entourage, circa 1976. L–R: guitarist Tommy Morell, pianist Mickey Laverine, office manager Joe Grant, Sammy, and my brother, drummer Ray Porrello, Jr.

Me, my brother, and my father with Sammy in his dressing room at the Front Row Theater in Cleveland, 1979.

Sammy entertains friends in his dressing room at the
Front Row Theater.

Jack Sheldon and his all-star jazz group performing at
the Hofbrau Haus in Las Vegas, December 1979.
L–R: Mundell Lowe, Nick Ceroli, Ray Brown, Jack
Sheldon, and Jimmy Cleveland.

Louie Bellson and his big band perform at the Louie Bellson & Slingerland Drum Co. National Drum Contest finals at the University of Nevada, Las Vegas, December 1979.

The winner and finalists of the Louie Bellson & Slingerland
Drum Co. National Drum Contest.
L–R: Me (4th place), Todd Strait (2nd), emcee Wayne Newton,
Hank Guaglianone (winner), Jim McCarty (3rd). Las Vegas, 1979.

At the drum contest: my drum teacher Ed Bobick, me, Louie
Bellson, my sister Susan, and my father, Ray Porrello, Sr.

CHAPTER

11

Ray had been traveling the world—China, Mexico, Australia—where Sammy recorded a live album at the iconic Sydney Opera House. I often practiced to it and tried mimicking some of my brother's licks.

Most recently, while Ray played Sammy's musical, *Stop the World–I Want to Get Off*, I was plodding through high school. I excelled in social studies and English but struggled with math. My enthusiasm for learning tanked, except in the music department. Dating was sporadic since Friday and Saturday evenings were reserved for gigs. By then, I was playing in several small jazz groups and a couple of big bands.

Most of the musicians I worked with knew my brother. I was often introduced as "Ray's brother," but it didn't bother me. They were veteran players in their forties and fifties. I felt a bit out of place, but the feeling quickly faded. Despite differences in age, race, gender, or ethnicity, there was a certain musicians' kinship. At sixteen, the pay was good—fifty or sixty dollars for a three-hour or four-hour gig. Following my father's advice, I opened a Local 4 credit union account and started saving for a car.

The small group jobs were low-key. I was comfortable from the first note but soon realized I was always the first to arrive and the last to leave. We played corporate dinners, union events, political rallies, outdoor concerts, clambakes, and government gigs. The big band jobs—mostly dinner dances—were more challenging because I had to read music. But drum lessons, my high school music education, and lots of practice prepared me well. A few times, I played shows with a conductor, including at the Policemen's Ball. Most often, I played wedding receptions at the city's top party centers.

After a year of playing on weekends, I saved enough money for a down payment on a car. I wasn't particular, wanting only one with air conditioning, an FM radio, and space to fit my drums. A two-year-old chocolate brown Oldsmobile Cutlass with a beige Landau top caught my eye. I got a loan from the Local 4 credit union. My father provided the required co-signature.

The day after I drove my car home, I hand-washed it and waxed it using the Simoniz and Turtle Wax that my brother had left behind. Inside the house, the police radio chattered away as usual. I got an idea, swung by Radio Shack, and bought a handheld police scanner. Now that I was driving, I could listen to police calls on the road. But that's not all I did. Anytime I was near a serious crime in progress, I was the wannabe cop who couldn't resist the urge to help if possible. I was hooked. Mostly, I just observed. But one time, I flagged down officers and pointed them toward a stolen car. I did the same thing when two armed robbers hit a Fotomat camera store.

One afternoon, an out-of-breath officer radioed that he was closing in on a burglary suspect who fled on foot. I was a block away when I noticed another cop running. He was carrying a shotgun.

Without thinking, I pulled to the curb and shouted, "I'll give you a ride!"

I moved my scanner off the passenger seat and the officer was in my car in a flash, having maneuvered his shotgun upright and between his legs. Not another word was exchanged. I sped him down the street and stopped quickly. He jumped out as sirens wailed in the distance. Bystanders were watching another cop pointing a shotgun at the suspect, who was lying on the ground.

A woman ran up to them, her voice breaking. "Don't shoot him; he's my son!"

I pulled a few houses ahead and got out to watch. The sirens grew louder and then stopped as two other police cars quickly approached, one skidding to a halt. The drama ended when officers handcuffed the young man.

Not all my efforts to play cop were successful. Late one quiet evening, I was out not far from my house. Suddenly, the scanner came to life. A burglar alarm at *Sound on Wheels*. I was right in front of the car audio shop. A patrol officer answered the call, and he gave his location.

Surely he won't make it here for several minutes.

I wheeled my car into the lot and stopped. From the driver's seat, I looked at the front windows. There was no movement inside.

What about the rear? Do I have time?

I pulled around the back of the shop and drove slowly. Nothing. I turned the corner to the front lot.

Okay, I have to get out of here.

As I headed for the exit, I was met by a speeding police car coming to a sudden stop. The officer blocked the exit. My inspiration turned to dread. Suddenly, my car was lit up by a thousand watts of light.

That's it. I'm going to jail.

My heart was racing. He got out, flashlight in one hand, revolver in the other, but pointed down at his side. I put my hands up high on my steering wheel so he could see them easily. He approached my window. Before he spoke, I started rattling off my explanation.

"Officer, I'm sorry, I'm interested in police work, and I have a police scanner, and I was right here when I heard the call, and I thought I'd take a look, but I didn't see anything and was just leaving." I took a breath.

With sweeps of his long black flashlight, the policeman looked curiously inside my car. The beam paused on my scanner and then went back to my face.

"Turn it off."

I turned off my ignition.

"The scanner," he said firmly.

I reached slowly to turn off my scanner, feeling the weight of my own stupidity, then faced forward again, squinting to avoid the light.

"Officer, I know it was stup—."

He interrupted sharply. "What's your name? Let me see your driver's license. Is this your car?"

I handed him my driver's license and answered his questions. He reholstered his gun, and I felt a little relief. Taking several steps away from my car, he started talking on his portable radio. Meanwhile, another police car arrived and pulled into a second driveway. That policeman got out, peered in the store with his flashlight, then got back in his car and went around toward the rear. A half minute later, he came back around, pulled out, and left. The first officer stepped back to my window. He was looking at me as he pointed to his holstered gun.

"You see this? Do you know what a bad decision you made? Do you know what could have happened?"

I knew he wasn't expecting an answer. He continued. "Here I am responding to an alarm drop and you're pulling out heading for the exit. What am I supposed to think? Not smart, kid."

"I know, I know, I'm sorry."

The officer handed me my driver's license and told me I could go. I thanked him and waited for him to pull away.

How could I be so stupid?

The officer pulled away and left. My house was in the same direction, and I was uncomfortable following him. My ego and passion for helping the police tanked. A mile later, he finally turned, and I continued straight to reach my street. I made a decision to stop carrying my police scanner in the car. That lasted three days.

CHAPTER 12

In 1980 I graduated from Cleveland Heights High School. With that milestone came a career choice. I was an eighteen-year-old drummer with no plans for the near future. My interest in police work had intensified over the past few years, but you had to be at least twenty-one to become a cop.

Under self-imposed pressure to pursue a career more acceptable to my parents, I registered for the electronics program at Lakeland Community College. I started in the fall. The initial courses were all math. I couldn't cut it. Beyond basic high school arithmetic, my creative brain just wasn't wired for numbers.

By the end of the year, my brother had enough of life on the road. After five-and-a-half years as Sammy Davis Jr.'s drummer, he decided to quit the show. His resignation was much to the disappointment of my father, a retired drummer with stars in his eyes. And the stars were his two sons. Ray played his last show in Honolulu, where Sammy appeared for five nights ending on New Year's Eve at the Hilton Hawaiian Village. Ray settled in Las Vegas and bought a house.

***

The calendar had just flipped to 1981. I brought my tuxedo and the shirt I wore for my New Year's Eve gig to the dry cleaner and returned home. It was about 1:00 in the afternoon when the telephone rang. The caller was George Rhodes, musical director for Sammy Davis Jr. He wanted to speak with me. My heart started racing as I stretched the phone cord and turned off the police radio. I didn't know it then, but before Ray quit, he asked George to consider me as his replacement.

"Your brother told me you're a good reader and can cut the show," Mr. Rhodes said in a deep, laid-back voice.

He explained that Sammy had a three-night run coming up in Minneapolis, and I could audition there. I said yes right away. He told me he'd call back with more details. After we hung up, my mind took off. I called my father at his office. He was just as excited as I was. For the next hour and a half, I couldn't concentrate on anything. All I could do was picture how the audition might go.

Two hours later the phone rang again. Mr. Rhodes said the show was at the Carlton Celebrity Room Theater on the weekend of January 16. He told me a plane ticket would be waiting at the airport. I had a question.

"Mr. Rhodes, will I sit in at a rehearsal?"

"Call me George. No, babe," he said. "You've got the job for three nights. You'll play the shows. Do you have a tuxedo?"

I was stunned, but I kept it together. "Oh, okay, thank you, Mr. Rhodes. Uh, yes, I have a tux."

"Good. I'll see you in Minneapolis."

We hung up and I just sat there.

No rehearsal? No warm-up? I was going to play the shows—for three nights?

When my father got home, we talked it over. We were thrilled, but he had a word of caution.

"Let's keep this quiet—just between us—until we see how you do in Minneapolis."

It was good advice.

***

I had ten days to get ready. The day after George called, I phoned two bandleaders to cancel three gigs I had for the week-end I'd be gone. I worked on the Rogers double-bass drum set that Louie Bellson had given my brother. When Ray got a second set, he left the Rogers drums at my parents' house, and I'd been using them for big band gigs. While my mind drifted, imagining the audition, I replaced the heads, checked the hardware and polished the white marine pearl finish to a gleam. Next, I dug out the heavy travel cases buried behind boxes of percussion gear and records.

I picked up my tuxedo from the dry cleaner. Back home, I went up to my brother's old bedroom. I only had one tux shirt, but Ray had left a few behind, and our sizes were close. They had ruffled fronts in pastel shades. I chose a light green one. Ray's old travel steamer was on his dresser, and I grabbed it and dusted off an old suitcase. I started packing about a week early—so I wouldn't have to rush.

CHAPTER 13

My father was upbeat and eager to help me pack. You might have thought it was his audition. Black travel cases protected the drums. They were thicker and stiffer than the black vinyl zip-up covers I used for local gigs. Still, they fit easily in my father's gray Lincoln Mark III. I said goodbye to my mother, pulled on my winter jacket, and got in the passenger seat. Thirty minutes later, Dad turned into Cleveland Hopkins International Airport. He found an opening in the busy departures area and pulled to the curb. When we opened the back doors and trunk to unload, an attendant noticed the drums. We helped as he moved everything onto a big luggage cart, checked my ticket, and tagged each case. My father handed him two dollars, and he maneuvered the cart away.

I turned to my father. "Thanks, Dad, I'll see you."

"I'm gonna wait with you."

At eighteen, I was eager to be on my own, but I didn't argue when my father insisted on waiting. I grabbed my suitcase and suit bag and went inside. He left to park the car. By the time I registered at the ticket counter and obtained a boarding pass, my father had returned. We went through the security checkpoint, walked to the gate, and sat down.

Dad handed me five or six one-dollar bills. "Make sure you tip the drivers and red caps."

Then he gave me a twenty-dollar bill to supplement my own cash. I thanked him and continued thinking about what essential items I may have forgotten. I observed the people around us, wondering where they might be going.

"Are you nervous?" my father asked.

"A little."

"Remember. Thunder! Push the band. Just play like you do in the basement."

I nodded, but at that moment, my anxiety wasn't caused by the upcoming audition. It was only my second time on an airplane, the first being the national contest two years earlier. The gate agent announced that my flight was boarding. I stood up. Dad wished me good luck. I knew he meant for the audition and not for the flight.

Just before he turned to leave, he said, "Have a good flight."

I walked through the jetway tunnel with several other passengers. A flight attendant greeted each of us at the door to the airplane. I had an aisle seat and a middle-aged couple was in the center and window seats.

I watched the safety demonstration, glanced around for the nearest exit and then reviewed the emergency information card. As we taxied to the runway, I listened intently to the captain's announcements. When we stopped, I looked out the window into the grayness of the Cleveland winter.

The sound of the engines increased to a muffled roar as we started to take off. The acceleration and pressure from the steep climb triggered a rush of adrenaline that cleared my sinuses. As we continued to gain altitude, I wiped a few beads of sweat off my forehead, adjusted the overhead fan, and turned it on full blast. Leveling out eased my stress. I glanced around at the other passengers and flight attendants and took a quick peek out the window at the sky, the clouds, and the earth below. I put my head back and closed my eyes as questions flooded my mind.

What will Sammy Davis, Jr. be like? What will George Rhodes be like? Can I cut the show? If I can't, I know I'll never get a second chance. And who are the red caps?

Flight attendants brought beverages and I asked for a ginger ale. The couple next to me got coffee. It was a dinner flight and I selected the chicken option over the beef. It was a chicken breast in a mushroom sauce with a side of cut green beans, a miniature salad and a fruit cocktail for dessert. After the trays were cleared, they came around again offering drink refills. I passed on more ginger ale. The man and woman beside me asked for more coffee. Shifting slightly in my seat, I stayed still, uneasy, as the flight attendant leaned over with a stainless steel pot. My eyes followed it as she poured.

The flight landed smoothly in Minneapolis early in the evening. George had said someone would pick me up, but when I scanned the crowd, no one seemed to notice. I followed the signs to baggage claim, watching travelers move confidently past me.

I arrived at the luggage carousel and recognized many of the faces from my flight as they emerged from the crowd to pull their bags off the conveyor. As they did, an airport employee quickly approached. He compared claim ticket numbers to luggage tags to ensure that passengers retrieved their own property. The conveyor snaked around numerous times before my things finally appeared. I pulled them off one by one, checking that all six drum cases were there.

I waited near the baggage claim area, watching for my ride. Ten minutes passed. I decided to move to the arriving passenger area. A porter in a uniform and wearing a red hat saw me looking around and offered to help. He brought over a big cart, and we loaded my drums and luggage on it. I followed him to a spot by one of the doors to the outside passenger pickup area. He said I could leave my things on the cart, so I smiled, thanked him and handed him two dollars. He thanked me and I watched him walk away.

Ah. A red cap.

I waited. Fifteen minutes passed without my ride coming. I began to worry.

I'll roll the cart back inside, then try to find a payphone close enough so I can keep an eye on my drums and luggage. Then I'll call the Registry Hotel and try to reach George Rhodes.

But for now, I would just wait.

Ten more minutes passed, and then a van with writing on the side approached. When it got close, I saw it was from the Registry. The driver, perhaps two years older than me, got out.

"Hope ya haven't been waitin' long."

"No," I said. "I just got here."

We loaded my drums, and I climbed into the passenger seat. The driver didn't know if he was supposed to take me to the hotel or the theater. I opted for the hotel. It was a ten-minute ride.

"You can leave your drums in the van until you figure out what to do," he said.

I entered the Registry Hotel lobby and spotted George Rhodes sitting in a chair, relaxed, with two other men. I approached, and it was apparent that he recognized me because of my resemblance to Ray or because I looked like a young, nervous musician. Probably both. I extended my hand.

"Mr. Rhodes? I'm Rick Porrello."

He smiled, remained seated, and gripped my hand firmly. "Hello, Ricky. Call me George."

George introduced me to Murphy Bennett, who wore a big, friendly smile, and Bernard Wilson who did not. George suggested that I bring my drums to the theatre and set up for rehearsal at 11:00

in the morning. The van driver took me to the Carlton Celebrity Room, which was just a few minutes away. He helped unload, and I handed him two dollars. In the theater, a heavy-set man was assembling music stands. I approached. He pointed me toward the drum riser, which was at the center of the bandstand. After setting up my drums, I returned to the hotel.

CHAPTER
14

At the Carlton Dinner Theater, George called a rehearsal break. Most of the musicians left the bandstand. The two-thousand-seat house was empty except for a few employees moving about. I didn't see Sammy. The bass player also stayed on the stage. I turned to my right and introduced myself. His name was Gary Raynor and he was a house player. Sammy's previous bassist was no longer with the show and was not yet replaced. Gary was tuning his acoustic bass and his bass guitar stood at the ready.

The drum book, a menacing three inches thick, lay on my matte black heavy-duty upright stand. The cover was labeled in the middle with bold letters: SAMMY. And in a smaller font near the bottom: Ray Porrello. I used my snare drum like a desk. Page by page, I flipped through the arrangements on the song list. I was familiar with several, thanks to one of Sammy's albums that my brother was on and to which I practiced. They included *Where or When, New York, New York,* and *Bye Bye Blackbird.*

I mentally noted rhythm cues, tempos, and time signatures and scrambled to review endings, watching for holds and cutoffs that would be directed by George. In several charts, there were penciled-in revisions or written instructions. I recognized my brother's printing on some of them. By this time, my head was a jumble of notes and cues. I realized that trying to familiarize myself with so many arrangements in fifteen minutes was futile. Sweat was beading on my forehead.

George called the band back and rehearsed several more songs— *For Once in My Life*, Send in the Clowns, a medley of *This is the Life* and *Hey There*, and one of Sammy's tap dance tunes, *I Can Do That*. In the middle of one song, I glanced across the room toward the lobby and saw Sammy walk in. He was wearing a cowboy hat and was accompanied by Murphy Bennett, Shirley Rhodes (whom I knew was George's wife), and two men I didn't recognize. Sammy came up on stage, hugged George, and greeted the band.

Sammy was right next to the rhythm section when I heard the guitarist say, "Good morning, Mr. D."

Sammy didn't acknowledge me directly—and I wasn't particularly disappointed. During his brief fifteen-minute visit, he rehearsed only one tune with the band, mostly so the soundman could adjust his microphone and monitors. Then he left with the same group he'd arrived with.

After another three songs, George started wrapping up the rehearsal. "Also, guys, take a look at *Lover Play On*. We'll bring Sammy on with that, so keep it at the top."

After rehearsal, Sammy's personal musicians invited me to accompany them back to the Registry in the hotel shuttle van. The next few hours flew by as I reviewed the music in my head. After showering, I headed to the hotel restaurant, where I was still processing the rehearsal. Sammy's guys were already seated and relaxed: lead trumpeter Fip Ricard, pianist Mickey Laverine, and guitarist Frank Accardo. I wasn't very hungry, so I just ordered a sandwich. While we waited for our food, they asked questions about my background and how Ray was doing. I asked Frank about the cylindrical device on his amplifier, and he told me it was a fan. When the checks came, Fip, Mickey, and Frank signed them to their rooms. I did the same. Before we left, Fip said a shuttle van would leave at 7:00 to take us to the theater. I steamed my tuxedo and shirt, got dressed, then it was back to the theater. Sammy was scheduled to perform two shows, at 8:00 p.m. and 11:00 p.m., for each of the three nights. There was no more rehearsing. It was showtime.

***

My jaw was tight as I anticipated my solo in *Every Little Beat Helps*. George's voice roared through the monitors:

"On drums, Ricky Porrello."

I built my solo of about ninety seconds to a climax of bass drums and cymbals in the style of Louie Bellson.

Following the overture, Sammy was introduced, and it seemed to me like his first show just flew by. Despite my anxiety, I felt like I made it through okay. During the second show, Sammy introduced comedian Bob Melvin, who looked to be about sixty. The curtain came down behind him and in front of the band.

"How 'bout that drummer?" I heard him say.

Oh my God. He's talking about me!

There was some light applause, and he continued. "I've got socks older than him."

I was more relaxed for the second show. Afterward, Fip, Mickey, and Frank were chatting with the house musicians who were packing up. While I was putting my music back in order, George motioned to us. "Sammy wants to see us." We followed him into Sammy's dressing room. I noticed Shirley Rhodes and Murphy Bennett.

Sammy immediately walked up to me, smiled and extended his hand. "You're a bitch of a drummer."

It was the best thing anyone had said to me since I arrived in Minneapolis, and it hit me like a wave of relief. There was some laughter as everyone smiled in approval. I thanked Sammy and shook his hand firmly. He handed George, Mickey, Frank, and me red silk handkerchiefs. He didn't specifically say that I was hired, but I took his compliment and the handkerchiefs as a welcome. Sammy invited everyone to have a drink. I took a deep breath.

This is it. I'm hired.

Shirley Rhodes stationed herself behind the bar. Fip got a whiskey, and Mickey and Frank got glasses of wine. I asked for a ginger ale, thanked Shirley, and moved off to the side. George joined me. He said he was impressed with my playing, especially during the rehearsal when Sammy walked in. "A lot of time," he explained, "when musicians first see Sammy, they tense up, and their playing suffers."

The next afternoon, George called me into his room. It was a suite—much bigger than the room I was in. I glanced around for Shirley but didn't see her. We sat down, and George explained the details of working with Sammy. He used a piece of hotel stationery to write out an informal contract:

"Weekly salary $600.00; Transportation and hotel included; You pay extras - food, phone, laundry, etc.; Extra pay for recordings or T.V. shows; Pay for overseas engagements starts the day you leave U.S.A. Instruments to be transported from and to the stage and stored at Mr. Davis' residence while off."

George said the road musicians traveled with Sammy about thirty weeks per year. They did not get paid when they were off. Then he turned to me with one last concern. "I'd like a gentlemen's agreement that you'll stay with us for at least two years."

"Sure, George."

"And after one year, Sammy will give you a raise."

I thanked George, we shook hands, and I returned to my room, where I called my father.

"I knew you could do it," Dad said.

The next day, I had a late breakfast in the hotel restaurant. A few of the crew and musicians were milling about.

Earl "Jolly" Brown, Sammy's hefty and sometimes-gruff-sometimes jovial stage manager, greeted me, "Hey, New Boy."

After breakfast, I went back to my room and reviewed Sammy's music arrangements. Following the engagement at the Carlton Dinner Theater, Sammy had two weeks off. Back home, my mother was glad for me, but I could tell she had mixed emotions. She worried I was too young for life on the road and questioned the financial security of a music career. She really wanted me to attend college.

"You have to have something to fall back on."

It was advice she repeated to me and my brother over the years.

CHAPTER 15

My father had to be the happiest dad in the world, and he wasted no time spreading the word. He had already called Louie Bellson, who was thrilled. Dad told me Louie said that if I hadn't gotten the job with Sammy, he would have recommended me to Tony Bennett.

At home, I bought drumsticks and drum heads from our friends at Academy Music Shop. The next day, I got two tux shirts and also bought a fan like the one Frank Accardo used on his amp. When I ran into friends and relatives, they congratulated me. Willy Lewis, the custodian from Local 4, came to our house to replace some locks for my father. When we were alone, he took out a paper bag from his tool container and said it was for me. I peeked inside and immediately felt a flush of embarrassment.

"Don't open it now," he said. "When you're out on the road meeting women, you gotta be prepared. You gotta be careful." Willy's face was serious, like a father offering advice to his son. I thanked him.

A few days later, the same general subject came up when I saw a police officer I knew in the high school parking lot.

"Keep it in your pants!" It felt less like advice and more like an order.

My latest examination in the mirror dictated that I would have to start shaving. At least weekly. I bought an electric shaver and tucked it into my suitcase with a new toothbrush, toothpaste, my little Instamatic camera, a pen knife I sometimes carried in my pocket, and, of course, Willy's gift.

My second job with Sammy was at Harrah's Hotel and Casino in Reno, Nevada. The region was within view of the majestic snow-capped Sierra Mountain Range. Inside Harrah's, the bright lights, chings, dings, and rings of the slots and poker machines in the casino and the chatter of gamblers were almost overwhelming. But since I was under twenty-one, I was not allowed in a casino. Not legally.

Harrah's main showroom was called the Headliner Room. Backstage, there was a dressing room for Sammy's musicians. I learned this was the case with every venue. Fortunatas "Fip" Ricard, who was from Chicago like George, was the senior member of Sammy's musicians. He was fifty-eight years old and had a stint with the Count Basie band. Fip served as a go-between for George and Sammy's musicians, often relaying rehearsal times or transportation details.

On occasion he got impatient if I didn't immediately understand everything he just told me. "You're not listening," he'd say.

Most of the time, he was good-natured and, like the other entourage members, a teaser. Traveling musicians had to pay work dues to the local union. Fip coordinated this, collecting amounts from each of us based on the length of Sammy's engagement—from five dollars for a weekend to thirty dollars for two weeks.

George Rhodes split his time between Sammy's dressing room and his own, where Fip often sat with him. Sometimes, I passed by, and they pretended they were talking about me.

"Shhh, shhh, here he comes," George would warn.

Fip would break into laughter, punctuated by him slapping the nearest flat surface repeatedly. The two pals had other verbal shtick. During rehearsals, if George had an issue with the trumpet section, it might devolve into mock bickering, with Fip passing the buck in a high-pitched silly whine. "Well, George, you're the reductor!"

Pianist Charles "Mickey" Laverine was fifty years old and a resident of Reno, Nevada. He was constantly busy during shows, providing background "noodling" while Sammy chatted with the audience between songs. Mickey had to be ready at a moment's notice to accompany the boss on a ballad or provide him with a keynote before a song. He must have known a thousand tunes.

Frank Accardo, from Niagara Falls, New York, was a graduate of the prestigious Berklee College of Music. He was twenty-five years old and had been Sammy's guitarist for two years by the time I joined the band.

In the forty-five minutes before each show, we spent most of our time in our dressing room. Fip, with a mute in his trumpet, would blow warm-up exercises. Frank might strum his unplugged guitar and chat with Mickey until we made our way to the stage about ten minutes before showtime.

Sammy's opening act for the Reno gig was Cathy Carlson, a popular performer in Las Vegas lounges who had appeared on the *Jerry Lewis Muscular Dystrophy Telethon* and *The Tonight Show with Johnny Carson*. I liked her opening tune, *Everybody Loves a Winner*, the lyrics of which encourage one to pursue their dreams in spite of their fears.

After the first night in Reno, I called my parents to tell them about the gig. My father was eager to have a photograph of me with Sammy.

"And make sure George is in it," he instructed.

The next evening, I asked George if he'd arrange for the photo. I also spoke with Mary, the showroom photographer, a pretty blonde a few years older than me. With her black-and-silver sequined skirt and radiant smile, she had caught my attention on opening night. Mary said she would be ready when I needed her. While waiting to see Sammy, I chatted with a plainclothes security guard, a retired cop from Hawaii. But my mind strayed a little to black and silver sequins.

George told me Sammy was ready for the photograph. I quickly checked in a mirror and straightened my bow tie, though it didn't need straightening. I felt a burst of pride as I glanced at my red silk handkerchief, in momentary disbelief that I was working for Sammy Davis, Jr. I felt nervous as George opened the door to Sammy's dressing room—hallowed ground to me. Mary followed us in. Shirley Rhodes smiled big and greeted me.

"Hey, baby."

She had a round face and was dressed sharp. I learned that she worked as Mr. D's administrative assistant and ran his Beverly Hills office. Murphy Bennett, Sammy's road manager, was seated and also greeted me with a smile.

While Mary prepped her camera, we waited for Sammy. I panned the scene like a video camera—a dark-paneled reception area with the feel of a cozy living room, a light-colored sofa, and two upholstered chairs. There was a coffee table with a bowl of fruit, some magazines and newspapers, a pack of Marlboro cigarettes, and a bar of Toblerone chocolate.

Mr. D emerged from an inside door—his private dressing and makeup area. He posed with me and George. I ignored the giggling in the hallway as Mary snapped two quick shots. I thanked Sammy and George before heading to the door, just as Shirley opened it to greet several visitors. The group included a half dozen gorgeous young women who looked to be in their twenties. They were dressed suggestively. And what they were suggesting was apparent. They filed in, brushing past me as I tried to maneuver through. Then I felt a pinch on my butt. I turned around, surprised, to find one of them grinning at me, her eyes wide with mischief. I shot her a smile before the door clicked shut behind me.

Later, Mary brought me two 8x10-inch copies of the photograph. While reaching for my wallet, I asked her how much they cost.

"Mr. Davis already paid," she said.

"He did?"

"Yeah, he said it's a gift to you," she said, smiling. "And he tipped me really well."

"Great, Mary."

Later, I asked George to thank Mr. D for me, and then I asked about the group of young women. Shirley was standing nearby. When I told George that one of them pinched my ass, he and Shirley burst into laughter.

"What say, Ricky?" Shirley asked with raised eyebrows. "She pinched your ass?"

George chuckled again. He explained that the girls were prostitutes from a well-known brothel located in an adjacent county where sex-for-hire was legal. It was called the Mustang Ranch. The owner, Joe Conforte, was friends with Sammy. Shirley shot me a hard look. "Ricky, you stay away from them girls."

Meanwhile, I heard that the house bass player, Phil, was a pilot. I was curious and asked him. He told me he flew gliders and offered to take me for a ride. Two days later, we went up. After we disengaged from the tow plane, it was eerily silent, and the flight was smooth. Then it got choppy. I was getting queasy and hated cutting the flight short, especially since I paid fifty dollars, but I told Phil I was done. He circled to the airport while I quietly took deep breaths.

Whatever you do, don't puke in the cockpit.

Phil brought us down to a gentle landing and explained that weather and terrain could cause turbulence, even for gliders. It took a half hour for my stomach to settle.

***

I was nearly done setting up my drums in New Orleans when I recognized the bassist. It was Gary Raynor from the Minneapolis show. He had told George that he was interested in the vacant position. A few weeks later, he was hired.

I was no longer the newest musician, but Jolly Brown still called me New Boy. He was forty-two. In his earlier years, Jolly was a stuntman and appeared as an extra in the James Bond film *Live and Let Die* as one of the villain's henchmen who tumbles over a deflating sofa.

In New Orleans, Fip, Mickey, Frank, Gary, and I walked around the famous French Quarter, stopping to watch street performers, including remarkably agile teenage break dancers.

One evening, Sammy took the whole entourage to a famous restaurant called Broussard's, a five-star dining icon dating back to 1920. Several of the guys were talking about oysters on the half-shell. Soon, trays of oysters on ice appeared. I loved shellfish but never braved raw oysters. Fip and Jolly coached me on how to prepare them: a squeeze of lemon juice, a dab of horseradish, and a drop or two of Tabasco sauce. Put the shell up to your lips and suck all that briny goodness into your mouth. I have been a fan ever since.

After New Orleans, Sammy was off for a few days. My father suggested that I get personalized bass drum heads. He bought me blank heads, and we visited a sign maker he knew. Dad explained to him that we wanted SAMMY in block letters in the center of the bass drum heads and my initials in a smaller font, above and off-center. Meanwhile, my father solicited interest from the *Cleveland Plain Dealer* newspaper. They decided to write a story about me and my brother. The reporter came to the house and got commentary from the whole family. He asked my mother about raising two drummers.

"After all these years," my mother said, "I miss it when I don't hear one of my sons practicing."

My sister joked, "I wonder if Sammy Davis needs a secretary."

A few days later, the story came out. It was titled "Sticking Together – Drummer Gets His Brother a Place in the Limelight with Sammy Davis." It included a photograph of Ray on his drums when he worked with Sammy and one of me at home on the drums. Getting a story and my photo in the newspaper was a terrific feeling. Family and friends congratulated me. My father's business associates mailed him copies of the article with notes of praise.

One afternoon, the police scanner chattered quietly on the living room table. Through the front window, I could see the mail had come. There was an envelope for me from Sammy's office. Every few weeks, they mailed an updated itinerary, and this was my first. I opened it eagerly. At the top, it said "Sammy's Roadrunners." Among several additions was a March 10th benefit in Atlanta, Georgia. The goal, I would learn, was to raise money to find a serial killer who had been murdering black children.

CHAPTER 16

My father and I went to pick up my new bass drum head, but when the artist showed it to us, Dad shook his head. I understood why. Before I could speak, my father said, "No, no, 'SAMMY' is too small, and Ricky's initials are too big."

We left. The artist revised his work. I picked up the heads a few days later and brought them to Florida where Mr. D had engagements in several cities. When George saw them, he gave me a thumbs-up and a smile of approval.

Sammy had two guests on his show—zany comedian Rip Taylor and pop and jazz singer Gerri Granger. The first show was at the Sunrise Theater in Fort Lauderdale. During rehearsal, George had us work on a Beatles medley that Sammy recorded a few years earlier. It opened with *Something*.

When we reached another tune called *With a Little Help from My Friends*, George turned his attention to me. "Ricky, play a Bo Diddley beat on this until we segue into..."

He stopped mid-sentence and chuckled, as did several musicians, at my wide eyes and gentle shrug. I knew of Bo Diddley, the legendary blues and rock & roll guitarist and singer, but I didn't know the beat bearing his name. My age and lack of experience were showing. George vocalized the simple beat, and the rest of the rhythm section joined him softly. I played along for a few bars, and we moved on.

The three nights in Fort Lauderdale went well, and my confidence grew. The morning after the last show, we had to leave by 9:00 a.m. I dragged myself out of bed and into the shower. The porters were busy, so I carried my luggage into the cool early morning and placed it with the rest next to our private coach. The bus would take us to the second Florida gig at the Bayfront Center Arena in St. Petersburg. I learned it was one of the few times the entourage traveled by bus instead of plane because Sammy usually didn't have multiple short engagements in such proximity.

I didn't see Sammy and assumed he was flying. Still half asleep, I took a seat toward the rear. I removed my sweat jacket, which I wore over my drum contest tee shirt, and bunched it up as a cushion between my head and the big window.

George, Shirley, and Rip Taylor sat in the front. Gerri Granger, petite and attractive, boarded the coach and joined them. The musicians spread out in the middle and back and were quiet. It was too early to socialize. Outside my window, Jolly, Dino, soundman Neil Shurmur and the other stage crew members loaded equipment and luggage into the cargo hold. There were new plastic tags with the letters TAEC on each piece. I learned it was due to a recent change in Sammy's management company, which was now called TransAmerican Entertainment Corporation. Jolly and Dino brought a half-dozen small cases and bags on the bus and piled them up on the two empty seats across from me.

A minute later, I was surprised to see Sammy board the bus. He was wearing a beige *Members Only* jacket, came down the aisle, and stopped by the small bags. "Good morning, Mr. D," I said.

"Mornin', babe."

I laid my head back against the window. Sammy removed his

jacket, revealing a revolver in a shoulder holster.

Damn. Mr. D is packin'.

He carefully stashed the gun and leather rig in a bag at the top of the heap. I would learn later about the threats Sammy had faced, especially in his earlier years.

An hour into the trip, the group started coming to life—especially loud, chatty and playful Rip Taylor, who was sitting next to Shirley. We were on a road parallel to the Atlantic when I mentioned to someone that this was the first time I had seen the ocean. Amidst all the chit-chat, someone told Sammy, and he instructed the driver to stop soon and "let the new boy see the water."

There was an ice cream shop up ahead, and our driver wheeled into a nearby parking area. I grabbed my camera, and we all filed out slowly and stretched. It had warmed up significantly. Several of us used the restrooms, and then Sammy treated everyone to ice cream. I laughed to myself when I saw big Jolly eating his cone, wearing a tee shirt that read, *Stay Hungry.*

Shirley made a fuss about me seeing the ocean. She ushered me over to big rocks just off the shore for a photo. Then George assembled everyone and took a group picture. While we finished our ice cream, Sammy briefly took the driver's seat to inspect the controls. Shirley was watching him, and I snapped a photo.

The stage crew members seldom called me Ricky. After New Boy got old, Jolly called me Sticks, Pale Face, Youngblood, or just Porrello. Frequently feeding off him was Neil Shurmur, Sammy's lanky, cowboy-type soundman and a fellow Midwesterner. Jolly called Neil "Mudbone," but I never knew why. Dino Meminger was Shirley Rhodes' nephew. To him, I was P-Baby. He had become Mr. D's lighting director and announcer. At the time, two brothers were working with Sammy's stage crew. John Giddens was about thirty-five, friendly, and laid back. Darrell was a few years older and aloof.

In St. Petersburg, backstage was dark when I arrived, so I asked a stagehand to turn on the work lights. While still in the dark, I continued searching for my drums. I found them among a bunch of cases of Sammy's equipment. I needed light to pull them out and start unpacking. After a couple of minutes, nobody had turned on the lights. Most of the workers were out in the house. There was another stagehand nearby, and I asked if he could have someone turn on some work lights. I waited a few more minutes. Still no lights. Then I started getting pissed. I needed about forty-five minutes to get set up for rehearsal, and it was too dark.

I walked onto the stage, looked out toward the house, and shouted rather heatedly, "May I please get some work lights turned on backstage?"

Darrell Giddens turned, started cursing at me, and quickly moved toward the stage. Before he reached me, Neil, who was on stage running cords, pulled him off to the side and calmed him. A minute later, the work lights went on.

"Thank you!"

While unpacking, I tried to figure out what had happened. I didn't know if Darrell had a personal problem or was just pissed at the new boy's centerstage announcement. But either way, he took the wind out of my sails for rehearsal. Later, I considered telling George about the incident, but I let it go.

Before the show, I had my camera with me when Gerri Granger came out of her dressing room. She looked stunning in a low-cut, shimmering dress.

John Giddens had the stage crew laughing when he joked, "Please let me touch one of 'em."

Gerri laughed, too. It was obvious that she had worked with Sammy before and was both confident and comfortable around the crew. I asked her if she would take a photo with me and she agreed. Jolly offered to take it.

"Give me your camera, New Boy."

He suggested staging the shot to make it look like Gerri and I got "caught" in her dressing room. She indulged him by giving me a wide-eyed hug.

I never understood what set Darrell off. But it didn't matter. He left Sammy's show, and soon after, his brother followed. I did miss John. Then Lester Mornay was hired. He was thirty-three years old and had been a publicist with Motown Records and *The Commodores*. Unlike many of the other stage crew members who were hired by Shirley Rhodes, Lester was hired directly by Sammy and became the assistant stage manager. Les often laughed at everyday annoyances within the stage crew. I probably spent as much of my free time with Lester and Dino, Sammy's lighting director and announcer, as I did with the musicians.

Dino was twenty-five years old, black, good-looking, and athletic. His self-confidence sometimes bordered on cockiness, but he had a sense of humor that balanced it out. Occasionally I joined him for a jog or a game of racquetball. One time we had just changed our clothes and headed for the court. Dino reached for the door and froze.

"Ricky, I can't go in there," he said, his voice suddenly serious.

I shrugged. "What's wrong?"

In mock seriousness he pointed to a sign on the door:

NO BLACK SOLES ON THE COURT!

***

There were fifteen members of Mr. D's entourage—five stage crew members, five musicians, and five staff members. The musicians and crew referred to Sammy's personal staff as A-Group: George and Shirley Rhodes, Murphy Bennett, Sammy's longtime friend and road manager, valet Bernard Wilson, and a bodyguard. The musicians and crew were B-Group. After flying to the next gig,

A-Group traveled by limousine. B-Group took hotel shuttles or taxi-cabs. When Sammy played a casino resort, he and A-Group stayed there. For most domestic engagements, B-Group was put up at a nice but less expensive hotel, like Holiday Inn or Ramada.

When Sammy performed in Nevada, his wife Altovise often visited. I sometimes saw Sammy's children, Tracey, Mark, and Jeff, who lived with their mother, Mr. D's first wife, May Britt. She was a former Swedish film actress. Sammy's high-powered attorney, John Climaco, a fellow Clevelander, sometimes showed up in a suit and cowboy boots. A few times, I saw Sammy's father. Once, he was walking through the casino looking sharp in a suit and tie. I noticed he was wearing a gold and diamond pendant that read, "Daddy Sam." The entourage also greeted Sammy's father as "Mr. D." Occasionally I caught glimpses of other celebrities, like the stunning Lola Falana, a longtime close friend of Sammy's.

And there was Sammy's biggest fan, a fifty-something Californian named Marilyn Walker. She'd attended Mr. D's night-club act for some twenty-five years. The night I met Marilyn, it was her 300th show.

***

I'd picked up the basics of playing a show—like positioning my music stand to see the conductor clearly. During the sound check, I made sure I could hear the bass player. In my first months, I learned a lot from George Rhodes and the other musicians. There were about one hundred and twenty-five arrangements in Sammy's music book. George saw me fumbling with the multi-page, folded arrangements by picking from front to back to find a particular number. He told me to grab one side from the rear of the stack and let the pages roll from back to front. It was much faster. Of course, this only worked when the arrangements had been previously returned to their proper order. As I got more familiar with Sammy's pacing, I recognized when I could return a completed chart back to its proper spot. When the show moved too quickly, I just slid a completed arrangement behind the pile or dropped it to the floor.

There were other lessons I learned. George stressed locking in tempo with the bassist. Early on, he'd sometimes interlace his fingers into a fist as a reminder. This focused synchronization between drums and bass was essential, especially when we played a slower tempo arrangement. For some of those tunes, George had the horns play in a laidback style, behind the beat Count Basie style. Trumpeter Fip Ricard kept the brass and reeds in the shadow of the rhythm section.

Maintaining a steady pulse is a cornerstone of drumming. The first time we rehearsed one of these tunes, I struggled with the subtle timing clash. I was too focused on the horns. George's admonition to lock in with the bass was the remedy. Later, when I analyzed recordings of Sammy's music, I could hear the irresistible groove that resulted from this nuance.

George also taught me to pace my playing. "Leave yourself somewhere to go," he said, meaning not to start a tune with too much energy or intensity.

When Sammy first called for a dance number, I was concerned about keeping time during his tap dance breaks. But I should've known better—he was Sammy Davis, Jr., a performer since age three, mastering both drums and tap dance—kindred rhythmic arts. My worries were unfounded, though I always maintained the meter mentally and softly with my foot through the tap dance breaks in case Sammy paused to make a quip.

A similar concern came the first time an arrangement included a section of half-time. As I was taught, half-time meant exactly that— half-speed, fifty percent of the tempo. Not with this group. "Always less than half," George instructed.

Whaaaat? Less than half? How much less?

The first few times an arrangement returned to the original tempo, it took more mental adjustment than just doubling the speed. Later, recordings proved to me that this musical nuance worked great for Sammy's hip, and swingin' style.

As I got more comfortable, I no longer felt compelled to keep my eyes glued to the music and to George. I started glancing around during the shows. On stage left, just out of sight of the audience, bodyguard DuWayne Rice, a former LAPD cop, kept a watchful eye on Sammy. A uniformed guard sat on stage right. Once in a while, I'd imagine myself jumping off the drum riser to defend Sammy from an attacker. It was thrilling—performing with a legend, playing to packed houses, and opening each show with the band. The first tune often featured several musicians, including an extended drum solo. My life had changed, and this was only the beginning.

My brother, drummer Ray Porrello, Jr.
with Sammy Davis, Jr. in 1979.

Me with Sammy and his conductor, George
Rhodes, in 1981. Photo by Mary McKinnon.

Posing with Sammy while taking pictures for the Slingerland
Drum Co. at Caesars Palace in Las Vegas, 1981.

George and Shirley Rhodes—Sammy's musical director
and executive secretary/manager, respectively.

With Sammy's stage crew. L–R: Me, Lester Mornay,
Dino Meminger, Jolly Brown, and Neil Shurmur.

"Caught" in the dressing room of Sammy's lovely guest star,
Gerri Granger.

Time out for a group photo by George Rhodes in Florida,
March 1981.
Standing L–R: Frank Accardo, guitarist; Fip Ricard, trumpeter;
Gary Raynor, bassist; Shirley Rhodes, business manager; John
Giddens, stage crew; Jolly Brown, stage manager; Murphy Bennett,
road manager; Mickey Laverine, pianist.
Kneeling: Comedian Rip Taylor, me, Sammy.
Courtesy of Eygie Rhodes.

CHAPTER 17

My brother got married, and I was his best man. When Sammy's Vegas gigs allowed, I'd stay with Ray and his wife instead of flying back to Cleveland. We spent time listening to music, running errands, cooking Italian food, and visiting with cousins and friends.

Ray worked with the Mickey Finn Show, a music-comedy troupe of stellar players founded by Fred Finn, and very popular at the Union Plaza Hotel. Ray also served as stick man for the Caesars Palace house orchestra for about a year.

During the early 1980s, there were seven full-time house orchestras that worked six nights a week at the major Vegas resorts. Two relief bands covered their days off. Additional full-time orchestras played the production shows like the *Folies Bergère* and *Lido*.

Sammy was performing at Caesars Palace in Las Vegas. It was my first time playing there. My father flew in for the occasion. Louie Bellson had successfully requested that Slingerland Drum Company give me a drum set because I was playing for Sammy. They shipped the double bass drum kit to Caesars. My cymbals were mostly hand-me-downs from Ray but included ones that Louie had given him. Dad hired a photographer and we asked Sammy to pose with me behind the drums. After the brief photo session, Dad stepped onto the drum riser.

He sat at the Slingerland set, smiled, and said, "I feel like a king up here."

During Sammy's engagement, a local reporter wrote about me and Ray in his *Las Vegas Jazz* column, mentioning my father's drumming background and Ray recommending me as Sammy's replacement. My father clipped the article and added it to his collection.

***

My only previous visit to Las Vegas had been for the drum contest. I knew little of the town and state. It began as a crossroads in the Mojave Desert, with a railway junction putting it on the map. In 1906, the Golden Gate Hotel and Casino opened on Fremont Street and still operates today. In 1931, the Nevada legislature legalized gambling as a way to regulate existing operations and discourage gaming profits from leaving the state.

The Hoover Dam was completed in 1935 to control flooding from the Colorado River, provide water, and generate hydroelectric power. Migration to the Southwest grew. By 1941, Vegas boasted more hotels, including the El Rancho, where a young Sammy Davis, Jr. performed with the Will Mastin trio.

Las Vegas is only a four-hour drive from Los Angeles. In the 1940s, a New York mobster named Benjamin "Bugsy" Siegel saw potential for profit. Using investment capital from pals like powerhouse Meyer Lansky, he started the construction of a luxurious hotel and casino. Siegel named it the Flamingo. A network of Cleveland mobsters, led by Moe Dalitz, followed with the Desert Inn. During the 1950s, mob leaders across the country invested in similar gambling resorts, including the Sands, the Stardust, and the Tropicana. Vegas was fast on its way to becoming an entertainment mecca. But Siegel mismanaged the mob funds and would not live to see the

Flamingo take off. In 1947, a sniper put a slug through Bugsy's head. That storied murder signaled the establishment of organized crime's iron-clad grip on Las Vegas. Out of the mobbed-up casinos and into the mob chiefs' pockets went monthly suitcases of "skim"—money stolen or "skimmed off the top" of casino cash receipts before being counted for taxation purposes.

During the years my brother and I worked for Sammy Davis, Jr., a ruthless mobster dominated Las Vegas street crime. Nicholas Pileggi's *Casino* tells the story of Tony Spilotro, the Chicago outfit's Vegas representative charged with keeping the stolen cash flowing uninterrupted from the Stardust. The story, dramatized in the hit movie of the same name, stars Robert De Niro, Sharon Stone, and Joe Pesci.

***

Jazz gained immense popularity before and during Prohibition. During the same period, a national crime syndicate—the Sicilian-American Mafia and a network of associated racketeers—was rising to power. With the mob's control of the liquor trade, many jazz nightclubs fell under their ownership or control. As a result, many of the most popular (and thus most valuable) jazz musicians, as well as former vaudeville performers, developed relationships with gangsters.

Frank Sinatra periodically downplayed his relationships with organized crime figures. However, his friendship with Chicago outfit boss Sam Giancana would become well-known. Sinatra likely introduced Sammy to the powerful Mafia leader.

"Gangsters wowed Sammy. As did real guns," wrote author Wil Haygood in his book *In Black and White.*

Sammy's friendship with Giancana ended in 1975, the year a hitman fired seven bullets into the mob boss's head while he was frying sausage and peppers.

Sammy continued his ties with the mob, needing cash to fuel his excessive spending. In *Gonna Do Great Things,* author Gary Fishgall wrote that Sammy started borrowing from Chicago mobsters in the 1950s. They paid his debts and gave him an interest-free loan of $100,000.

"In return, [Sammy] would have to pay over 20 percent of his earnings for fifteen years."

"[Sammy] wanted to throw money around the way Sinatra threw money around," observed Haygood. "Money for gifts, for clothes, for women... So he went tugging on the sleeves of nightclub owners."

By the late 1970s and early 1980s, Sammy was earning millions annually. Though less dependent on mob money, he still lived paycheck to paycheck, occasionally taking advances from his friend, Bill Harrah, the famed casino owner.

In Las Vegas during this period, Sammy frequently performed at Caesars Palace, packing its 800-seat *Circus Maximus* showroom. In 1981, a show with cocktails cost $30 per person. Showtimes were at 9:00 p.m. and 12:30 a.m. Most often, the musicians and stage crew—B-Group—stayed at the Ambassador Inn, just a mile from the Strip. It was the same place I stayed for the drum contest. The hotel had two floors of rooms overlooking a courtyard with a pool and jacuzzi. I started bringing my bathing suit and sunscreen for Sammy's Vegas gigs.

After shows, I was usually wired and hungry. Across from the Ambassador Inn was a pizza shop that stayed open all night. Sometimes, I phoned in a takeout order, perhaps a small pizza and buffalo chicken wings. The first time I walked in to pick up my food, I noticed the clerk wore a pistol on his hip. I'd return to my room, eat, and watch *Late Night with David Letterman*, often alone or with a B-Group member.

Staying up late and sleeping in became my routine. Neil Shurmur started calling me "Drac," teasing me that I kept vampire hours. Indeed it might be 11:00 a.m. before I'd be up and looking for breakfast. I'd hit the coffee shop where Top 40 hits played, and the waitresses knew us by name. At first I didn't go into the casino because I was underage. But as the months went by, I occasionally stopped at a corner slot machine and dropped a few coins.

CHAPTER 18

Sammy toured about thirty weeks out of the year. Other times he might appear on a television series or talk show, something not involving his entourage. His road engagements usually lasted a weekend, one week, or two weeks. He toured abroad several times per year. Sometimes, he did a one-nighter—like a telethon or other benefit. Sammy's generosity was never-ending, especially for causes benefiting blacks, Jews and children.

During my time with him, much of Sammy's touring schedule was spent at three gambling resorts in Nevada. He preferred the smallest venue—the Headliner Room at Harrah's Reno. Its seating capacity of 450 had more of a nightclub feel for him than the South Shore Room at Harrah's Lake Tahoe or the Circus Maximus at Caesars Palace in Las Vegas, each seating about 800. Lake Tahoe, in particular, was a favorite for the entourage. These venues were familiar and comforting, and we looked forward to being with friends—house musicians, stage crews, and casino staff.

No matter where the venue was, we'd check in and settle into our rooms upon arrival. Each member of the entourage got his own room. We'd run into each other in the lobby and often shared a table in the restaurant. I would check in with trumpeter Fip Ricard to find out the rehearsal time and when the musicians would be leaving for the theater. On the first day of each gig, there was a rehearsal, often at 11:00 a.m.

For Sammy's two-week engagements at Harrah's in Reno and Lake Tahoe, the house bands got one night off and were replaced by the relief band. That necessitated an additional rehearsal halfway through the gig. For the opening night rehearsal, I would get there an hour early to set up. At venues where Sammy performed often, we exchanged handshakes and hugs with familiar house players and traded wisecracks with our stage crew. Usually I found my equipment next to the drum riser. Now and then the stagehands were running behind, and I would have to do a little searching among Sammy's stage equipment. Next I would unpack the drums from their travel cases.

The drum riser was always in the middle of the band. To my left, facing the audience, was the trumpet section, elevated at the highest point with four players. In front of them, at the next level down, were the four trombonists. The drum riser was usually at this tier. And in the next row, at stage level, were the five saxophonists. To my right was the string section—four violins, two violas, and two cellos—often on two or three ascending risers. The grand piano would be in front of me at stage level. And to my direct left and right were the guitarist and bassist, most often on the same tier as me.

While I carefully set up my drums, Neil Shurmur and the house sound technicians ran dozens of long cords for microphones and monitors. They positioned microphones for each drum and my hi-hat. Two overhead mics covered my ride and crash cymbals. Lester, Jolly, and Dino passed out the music books, placing them on the corresponding music stands. The white stands were boldly printed with "SAMMY" and featured a black caricature silhouette of him in his Mr. Bojangles finale pose. Except for me and the percussionist, all the musicians used these low music stands. My drum set and the percussionist's instruments required heavy-duty telescoping stands.

Setting up my drums took about thirty minutes. My final task was to plug in my portable fan and position it on my left bass drum. I kept it on low throughout the show. By this time, Frank Accardo and Gary Raynor were starting to warm up. George Rhodes was in his dressing room.

Dressing rooms were usually down a long hallway. Individual rooms were assigned to the opening act, Sammy's musicians, and a large one for the house band. Occasionally the house band leader had a room of his own. Bernard Wilson often had a dedicated room for Sammy's wardrobe. The door was usually open, revealing a rack of Mr. D's clothes.

Bernard would be leaning over an ironing board, pressing a shirt or pair of pants to crisp perfection. A lovable, openly gay man in his late fifties, he called his male co-workers "Miss"—Miss Frank, Miss Mickey—and now and then in return, we affectionately called him Bernice. Bernard often appeared timid, as if expecting someone to yell at him. He was prone to sulky moods, especially if the boss was not in the best of humor.

"Don't bother Sammy, child," he might warn. "He's in a bad mood."

Bernard chuckled at his own humor, laughing hardest when I playfully batted away his hand from reaching toward my crotch as he pretended to brush off my pants. "C'mere Miss Ricky. You got some lint on your trousers."

"Get the hell outta here, Bernard."

Murphy Bennett, a Chicagoan, worked as a valet and traveling assistant for Sammy in the late 1950s. As the entourage grew, Murphy became his road manager and confidante. He screened

Sammy's phone calls, carried his cash, and greeted visitors backstage. When we were overseas, he cashed our paychecks. During shows, Murphy wore a suit and tie.

If I saw Mr. D arriving or departing with a few people, Murphy was usually trailing a few feet behind. His unhurried pace and the chain with a three-inch-long gold cross he sported led a few of the musicians to refer to him as Father Murphy. Sammy's shows always began with his theme song, *Murphy Here*. I never thought much about the song title until I'd been on the job for a few months.

One day backstage, Murphy answered a phone extension. "Hello, Murphy here."

Shirley Rhodes, George's wife, usually took up her post in Sammy's dressing room during performances. Unlike George and Murphy, who moved at a slower pace, Shirley was a dynamo.

***

Sammy often told his audience he wanted his shows to feel like a house party. No matter how he felt, he left his frustrations behind once he hit the stage. Instilled with an ethic from his uncle and dad, he always gave one hundred and ten percent. He was known for his lengthy performances. While forty-five minutes or an hour was the norm for a typical nightclub show, Sammy spent twice that much time on stage. And that didn't include his opening guest, who usually did a half hour.

Sammy's impromptu style electrified his shows, keeping every performance alive and unpredictable. His ability to improvise provided him the freedom to tailor each performance to his audience. It kept the musicians on their toes, but the unpredictability unnerved me, especially since I couldn't rely on a set list for my arrangements. Sammy would have informed George of his opening song and second and third selections. The opening tune would segue into the second, and the second song into the third. After the third tune,

Mr. D welcomed the audience, monologued a bit, and got a feel for the crowd.

Many of the subsequent songs were ones we had rehearsed. But sometimes Sammy unexpectedly called for a song that we had to "sight read." He might joke about the musicians suddenly digging through their music.

In the voice of an irritated old black man Sammy sometimes used on stage, he'd mock whisper, "Why can't that little turkey do the same show he did yesterday?"

When Sammy decided on a song, he'd either quietly inform George or just tell him outright: "George, let's do *Birth of the Blues*."

George would provide the chart number, though oftentimes you could tell where Sammy was headed just by listening to the monologue. His guys knew to tune in—if he mentioned his hometown, we knew *New York, New York* was coming next. We'd signal the players around us, but in Vegas, Reno, and Lake Tahoe, the musicians rarely needed cues. Sammy thrived on that freedom, which meant staying constantly alert was essential when working with him.

Sammy Davis, Jr.

Roadrunners

<u>A-Group</u>

Sammy Davis, Jr.

- George Rhodes, Music Director
- Murphy Bennett, Road Manager
- Shirley Rhodes, Business Manager
- Brian Dellow, Security Director
- Bernard Wilson, Valet

<u>B-Group</u>

Musicians

- Fip Ricard, Lead Trumpeter
- Mickey Laverine, Pianist
- Frank Accardo, Guitarist
- Gary Raynor, Bassist
- Rick Porrello, Drummer

Stage Crew

- Jolly Brown, Stage Manager
- Lester Mornay, Asst. Stage Manager
- Neil Shurmur, Sound Technician
- Dino Meminger, Lighting Director and Announcer

Jan. 1981 through June 1983

CHAPTER
19

During the first fifteen minutes of the show, Sammy would introduce George Rhodes as his longtime musical conductor—his man "at the helm of things." If a song immediately followed George's introduction, Sammy might add, "Now, George, wave your arms and see if the band follows you," and get a chuckle from the audience.

Sammy joked about it, but he and George had a profound connection on stage. When an arrangement required definitive conducting, George kept Sammy in his peripheral vision. In musical synchrony, he took cues from Mr. D's breaths, phrasing or movements, and translated them to precise direction for the orchestra.

George was sixty-two when I started drumming for Sammy in 1981. He had been working for Sammy for nearly thirty years. No doubt, his constant discreet presence on stage was a comfort for Mr. D. A Chicago native, George played piano for numerous well-known jazz artists early in his career. Under conductor Morton Stevens, he began work with Sammy as a pianist in the 1950s. After Morty left, George took over as Sammy's music director, and a new pianist was hired.

George moved slowly, with an easygoing temperament on and off stage. No matter the country or city, he had a good working rapport with the house musicians. But he meant business. You certainly didn't drink or talk on stage, and you always played your ass off, whether on opening night or twelve days into a two-week engagement.

During the first two nights of a gig, I was getting worried when George gave me his two-fisted signal to lock in with the bass player. I thought I had been. A few nights later, George called me aside. He revisited the importance of the drummer and bassist locking into a groove. It took me a few more shows to figure that I'd been watching George too closely, like a security blanket. I wasn't trusting my skill and timing, so I dialed up my attention to focus on myself— my sock cymbals in particular—and the bassist. Over the next few weeks, I improved my awareness of my timing. It's a crucial skill for all musicians, especially drummers—a subconscious time clock, a mental metronome running in the background like a computer program.

My confidence grew on and off stage. One evening, I stumbled over it. B-Group was staying in the same hotel as A-Group. One evening, George asked me if I wanted to order pizza to have with some of the other members of the entourage. I immediately said yes and offered to pay.

"No, Ricky. I'm buying."

I really wanted to treat the group to pizza. I pointed at George, smiled, and said, "I'm paying for it."

George shot me a serious look and I immediately realized my misstep. "Who do you think you are, Little Caesar?"

I quickly realized my misstep, but George cracked a smile at my overconfident offer. It was a reminder that George wasn't just one of the guys—he was the boss. We ate pizza. And George paid.

***

Sammy was famous for his spot-on impressions of entertainers. He'd launch into one if it fit his banter between songs. Most often he parsed them out to the tune *Rock a Bye Your Baby with a Dixie Melody*. He called the song the "national anthem of variety performers." Sammy, like many impersonators, exaggerated his subjects' appearance, mannerisms, and voices, stretching them to the ridiculous, like a caricature. He impersonated singers and actors like Tony Bennett, Nat King Cole, Dean Martin, Billy Eckstine, Mario Lanza, Jerry Lewis, and many others.

Sammy believed in equality—across race, gender, and culture. He made fun of everyone—whites, blacks, and most of all, himself. He laughed about aging out of his wild days when he wore groovy jumpsuits and cavorted with chorus girls. Now, custom suits and sportscoats with a tie were his stage apparel. Sammy joked about being too old for the modern hits. "C'mon, how would it look up here if I sang *Do Ya Think I'm Sexy*," he'd ask, referring to Rod Stewart's disco hit. He got a similar laugh when he joked about his small stature. "There's not enough of me to do the Village People's *Macho Man*." His audiences loved his superb blend of raw talent, charisma, self-deprecating humor, humility, and confidence.

Sammy joked about the ups and downs of his career and being a survivor. He had four hits. But for him, it wasn't enough. He made a joke of that, too. When he introduced *Candy Man, I've Gotta Be Me, What Kind of Fool Am I*, or *Mr. Bojangles*, he'd say he had to spread them out. "I sing one, wait a little while, do another, wait a little while."

Sammy transitioned from singing moving ballads to breakneck tempos in music arranged mostly by George Rhodes. He performed jazz standards, pop-rock hits, medleys, and Broadway numbers. Some of his arrangements started with just him and the rhythm section. We had to be ready to come in on the first beat if Mr. D suddenly turned and vocalized a distinct count-off. Then we'd play a vamp—a short, repeating phrase that serves as a musical placeholder.

"Ching chinga ching chinga," and just like that, we were into *The Candy Man* introduction. A crossover tune—a syrupy departure from his usual repertoire—the song reached No. 1 on the Billboard Hot 100 chart, earning Sammy a new following.

Now and then he'd tell the audience, "I sang this song for two years before I learned what candy man meant on the street corner," referring to the 1970s slang for a drug dealer. The audience would laugh, and Mr. D would start singing:

"Who can take a sunrise?.."

If Sammy vocalized a Latin-flavored rhythm, something like "gong-chicka-gong-ch'-gong-gong-ch'gong," it was to kick off his bossa and swing rendition of Ain't Misbehavin'.

"...I know for certain, the one I love, I am through with flirtin', it's just you I'm thinkin' of. Ain't misbehavin', I'm savin' my love for you..."

If Mr. D's count-off was at a presto tempo, it was probably for his bright and whimsical rendition of *That Old Black Magic*, performed with the rhythm section. Sometimes, Sammy sang a ballad accompanied only by Mickey Laverine's piano or, occasionally, by Frank Accardo's guitar.

During one show, Sammy turned to the rhythm section and counted off with a medium-slow "Unhh, Unhh, Unhh, Unhh," accenting each beat with his foot. I joined in with the rhythm section's vamp, unaware of the song until George discreetly held up the arrangement of *You're Nobody 'Til Somebody Loves You*.

As the other musicians pulled their copies, I flipped through my music with my left hand while keeping time with my right. George saw me searching. The arrangement was missing from my book. It was too late.

Sammy started singing. At "So find yourself somebody to love," I noticed that the band was about to come in strong. Sweat rolled into my eyes, but there was no time to panic. I could barely read the notes of the trombonist's music nearest me, but I did set up and catch most of the important figures. It was a trick that a bandleader taught me back home when drum arrangements were missing or, more frequently, lacking essential details.

As I struggled to see the trombone music, we reached the last line. It included several holds and breaks, all of which were conducted. I felt George was emphasizing his arm movements to help me, and I was relieved when he cut off the final chord. He nodded to me and gave me a slight smile.

As the applause peaked, I heard George mention to Mr. D, "Your drummer didn't have any music."

Sammy glanced up at me and quickly said off-mic, "Good job, Rick." The simple recognition by both of my bosses boosted my confidence.

When the god of spontaneity moved Sammy, he reprised a routine that harked back to the late 1950s with his first drummer, Michael Silva.

He suddenly turned to me. "Ricky! Ba-doon-doon-dee-gum, ga-diggety gohn gohn."

I immediately recognized the beat, turned to my floor tom-tom, and took it up. Mr. D had vocalized the enduring Gene Krupa rhythm from the 1937 hit *Sing, Sing, Sing*. A few seconds into the routine, a bright white light bathed the drum riser. I sat up an inch and put on a slight smile. In my peripheral vision, I noticed — with some unease — George slowly walking offstage and disappearing behind the curtain at stage left. It was just Mr. D and me. He started singing:

"Night and day, you are the one."

At the time, I had no idea, but *Night and Day* was Mr. D's

setup for a lengthy, free-form medley. It was two of the oldest musical instruments — drums and the human voice. Sammy performed whatever tunes or instrumental mimicry inspired him. He moved seamlessly from one song to the next, ad-libbing through a chorus of each—sometimes twelve or more tunes.

When Mr. D returned to *Night and Day*, I knew he was closing. He reached the final note, riffed on it, then swelled to a hatchet ending. The stage went black for a moment, then the lights came up brightly — along with hearty applause. I took a deep breath in and out.

I wish I had known that was coming.

Sammy interrupted my thought. "My drummer, ladies and gentlemen—Ricky Porrella. He's eighteen years old."

At the additional applause, I smiled and nodded and waved at the audience. With his New York City accent, Mr. D always pronounced the last letter of my name more as an "A" than an "O." It was the same with Frank "Accarda". George seemed to take notice. Whenever he introduced either of us, he articulated each syllable.

From time to time, Sammy played with the lyrics, tossing in his own twists to get a laugh. He stretched lines with rhythmic precision to match his interpretation or substitute words. He incorporated black references. He used Yiddish terms, as he did in *The Candy Man* from the movie *Willy Wonka & the Chocolate Factory*. The song tells the story of a candy maker with a talent for making everything so delicious that you could eat the dishes.

Sammy added his own touch, singing, "You can even eat the knishes."

Mr. D might spontaneously punctuate a line with his signature, cat-like scream. However, that ad-lib burst of spirit was more common in the 1960s and 1970s. Occasionally, he reworked entire lines, like in his rendition of *You're Nobody 'Til Somebody Loves You*:

"So all you sisters, go get yourself a brother, and the rest of you folks take care of one another. WEOOOW!"

For ninety minutes, Sammy delivered entertainment at its finest. He reveled in the smiles, laughter, and applause. It was love. He lived for it.

Sometimes an audience member shouted, "We love you, Sammy!"

Mr. D often answered, "Thank you, babe, that's a two-way street."

CHAPTER
20

March arrived and I was settling into my role in music, live entertainment, and travel. I was living a dream. But that month was a jarring reminder of life's brutality. Since the summer of 1979 in Atlanta, Georgia, bodies of murder victims, primarily black children and teenagers, had been turning up every few weeks. The investigation was hampered due to inadequate funding, so Sammy conceived a benefit show. He elicited Frank Sinatra's help. The two superstars sometimes participated in each other's charitable events. Sammy also invited actor Burt Reynolds. In 1980, they filmed a movie called *The Cannonball Run*, a comedy about a cross-country race.

I arrived in Atlanta two days before the show. George was in the hotel lobby. He invited me to attend a *Kool and the Gang* concert with him, Shirley, Murphy Bennett, and Bernard Wilson. The show was the following evening at Atlanta's Omni Coliseum. We were picked up in a limousine. *Kool and the Gang's* big hit, *Celebration*, had been number one on the *Billboard* chart for several weeks. The house was packed. George and Shirley were guests of a city official, so we got to sit in his loge.

It was late in the evening when the show ended. We were tired, mentally spent from the sensory overload of the concert and relieved to get to the limo. The driver slowly proceeded through the parking lot as we gazed out the windows at the crowd of thousands returning to their cars. Some of them peered curiously into our limo. I was the only white guy riding with black members of Sammy's entourage that night, and there weren't many other white folks at the show, either. It wasn't part of my inner dialogue; the entourage was more like a family. But Shirley Rhodes found the moment ripe for comment.

"Ricky must be thinking to himself, I ain't never seen this many niggers before," she said.

A roar of laughter rippled through the car.

I played along, yawned, stretched, and said, "I'm tired everyone. I think I'll lay down on the floor for a while," sparking a second wave of laughter.

***

The benefit took place at Atlanta's Civic Center. On the morning of rehearsal, I was on stage, tightening my cymbal stands. George was at his podium, looking over his music, when a man casually walked across the stage toward him.

Frank Sinatra!

It was my first sighting of the superstar and Mr. D's Rat Pack pal.

Hmm. He looks older than I expected.

Frank and George exchanged smiles and hugged. They chatted quietly for about thirty seconds when I heard George speak up:

"Have you met our new drummer, Ricky Porrello?"

Frank turned and looked up at me. I nodded and said, "Hello, Mr. Sinatra."

We exchanged a smile and a wave before he turned back to his conversation with George.

After rehearsal started, I noticed uniformed and plainclothes police officers mingling. A K-9 officer led his bomb-detection dog around the inside perimeter and up and down the rows.

Before the show, we were each given two-inch long green ribbons to wear on our lapels—symbols of remembrance for the victims. Shortly before the show began, I overheard someone say that the killer might show up at the benefit. Apparently, the rumor had been going around for a few days. Several cops were stationed backstage. Even stage manager Jolly Brown got in on the security action. Just before show time, I was near Sammy's dressing room when I heard lighting director Dino Meminger say, "Damn, Jolly!" I turned and saw Jolly smiling and holding his suit jacket open to show Dino his revolver in a shoulder holster.

At the top of the show, Burt Reynolds introduced Frank Sinatra, and Mr. D. Sammy muted the celebratory tendencies by speaking of the senseless violence, emphasizing the reason for the charity show. In the end, Sammy's benefit raised $150,000 for the investigation, but just three days later, another slaying occurred—a stark reminder of the ongoing tragedy. During the next two months, there were seven more. In June, a man was arrested and eventually convicted of two of the murders. He was also a suspect in most of the others and was convicted and sentenced to life in prison.

After we left Atlanta, we had much of April off. It was the period when a gunman attempted to assassinate President Ronald Reagan. The world was transfixed by coverage of the incident caught on news cameras. Two Cleveland labor union officials were right behind the gunman and assisted in wrestling him to the ground.

***

When in Las Vegas or between gigs, I spent some of my off time with my brother. We ran errands, cooked, and listened to music. If I had a date, Ray would let me borrow his car. Once in a while, my father flew in from Cleveland to join us. My cousin Tony, the one who always made sure I was properly attired for dinner as a boy, had recently moved to Vegas.

Ray, Tony, and I socialized with other relatives and friends who lived in Las Vegas. Getting together with cousins for homemade pasta dinners was a favorite activity. Playing the poker machines at Caesars Palace was another. Amidst the background of flashing lights and bells, we would sit at adjacent five-card draw poker games. We got skilled at feeding five quarters in quick succession for the maximum $1.25 wager. Occasionally, someone in a rush dropped a coin on the carpet. To add a laugh, Tony established a rule. The fumbler had to announce "quarter down," and then our group had to halt their play until the coin was retrieved. Sometimes, an adjacent gambler joined our antics and adopted the rule. Calling "quarter down" was almost as much fun as winning. And much more frequent.

When one of us depleted his supply, another who was up on his luck donated a handful of quarters. After all, the big jackpot might be just one more play away. When we all ran dry, we would wander through the casino, buy a few yanks from a slot machine, chat with friends or co-workers, or grab a meal.

Another time at Caesars, I ventured away from Ray and Tony. The floor buzzed with the chatter of players and dealers and the chinging of coins swallowed up by slot machines. I tried to keep a low profile since I was underage. Cocktail waitresses moved quickly, delivering free drinks to gamblers. The young women sported short white skirts and toga-like tops draped over one shoulder, leaving the other one bare. The public address system came to life, interrupting my thoughts.

"Paging Rick Porrello, please pick up a white courtesy phone. Rick Porrello, please pick up a white courtesy phone."

I knew it was coming. I was too young to be in the casino, and now I was in trouble.

I spotted one of the telephones on a wall and weaved through the crowd. When I reached the phone, I paused, thinking it might be better to ignore the page. I picked up the handset and identified myself. The operator made the connection.

"Hello," a voice said.

I strained to hear. "Who is this?" I asked.

"It's Tony."

"Where are you?"

"I'm over here."

I looked around and noticed a waving arm on the other side of the room. It was my cousin Tony. He told me he was calling from another courtesy phone and started laughing. "I thought you might like to hear your name."

One time, while my brother, Tony, and I were finishing a snack at the Caesars coffee shop, we ran into actor Greg Morris. Born in Cleveland, he co-starred in the original *Mission: Impossible* TV series. We introduced ourselves, and he was friendly. We had a few laughs, especially when Tony handed him a fork. "Greg, I locked my keys in my car. Can you get me in?"

***

My two-bass drum set with the white pearl finish gleamed under the stage lights. I'd gained confidence after four months of playing for Sammy. He was singing the *Birth of the Blues* while I played strong backbeats on my snare drum. Mr. D had the audience clapping as usual to the spirited and swinging arrangement. In sync with Sammy's movements, George cut off the last chord.

The applause was still strong when Mr. D started his usual reprise. "Keep clapping along," he told the crowd.

The song ended. Over the applause, Sammy said, "Anybody don't like that, don't like chicken on Sunday."

There were some scattered laughs. I was loaded and cocked for

Mr. D's next song, *Where or When*. The arrangement was one of my favorites. I liked the bold entrance in which the drums set up the whole orchestra to come in heavy as the stage lighting came up to full brilliance. I was mentally prepared for George's downbeat. When his baton came down, I set up a simple but commanding fill and cymbal crash for the orchestra's entrance.

Crash!

Wait. No full band? No lights?

I immediately heard the string section playing the soft vamp for *I Gotta Be Me.*

Wrong song!

Not even close. These tunes had different rhythms, time signatures, and contrasting introductions. Everyone in the orchestra knew *Gotta Be* was next. Except me.

How did this happen?

In an instant, I sank my volume and turned to my closed hi-hat. It took only one measure to recover as I locked in with Gary Raynor. I lowered my head slightly and put on my best poker face.

It's okay. We're all together and moving on.

I was dying inside.

My gaze was frozen straight ahead, but I saw everything. George's eyes were glued to his music as he struggled not to laugh. Guitarist Frank Accardo was smiling stiffly, also holding back a chuckle. At the piano, Mickey Laverine was trying to stop laughing. In the meantime, Sammy mercifully ignored my obvious blunder and came in as usual.

Whether I'm right, or whether I'm wrong

I dreaded the end of the show. George had to be pissed. And worse, probably Sammy, too. But I heard nothing from either. I think George knew I was conscientious enough to have learned a hard lesson to pay better attention. Of course, I was fair game with the musicians and crew as the teasing and jokes started.

CHAPTER
21

When I started working with Sammy Davis, Jr. in 1981, he was fifty-five. His wild days were mostly behind him. From the 1960s through the mid-1970s, he often sported jumpsuits or Nehru jackets. His repertoire included high-energy numbers like Bill Chase's *Get It On* and a Blood Sweat and Tears medley. His drug use—some marijuana or a little cocaine—was at a high. Sammy even offered the Hollywood drug of choice to house guests, placing a small crystal bowl of the white powder "next to the mixed nuts."

By 1980, Sammy had cut down on his consumption of alcohol due to liver damage. The swigs he took from his pewter mug during shows were of Coca-Cola or strawberry soda. Dr. Brown's was a favorite, heavy on the ice.

Sammy lived on Summit Drive in Beverly Hills. I was never in his house, but later learned it had two dozen rooms. The two-acre property was secured by surveillance cameras, and an armed guard who communicated with people inside via intercom. Several of Sammy's cars were parked in the circular drive, and the backyard featured a large pool. The living room had a sunken area with a built-in aquarium. Behind the bar was a wall of photos—Sammy with family and celebrity friends like John Wayne, Muhammad Ali, Liza Minnelli, Sam Cooke, Jerry Lewis, Elvis Presley, Jeff Chandler, Tony Curtis, and Janet Leigh. A recreation room included a pool table and firearms display. Sammy took pride in his collection of modern and Western pistols, as well as his collection of one thousand films and tapes.

On the road, Sammy spent much of his time in his suite and thus insisted on traveling with familiar comforts. As soon as he checked into a new hotel, his assistants unpacked numerous bags and cases. They hung his favorite photographs. The stage crew members were responsible for setting up television sets, video players, and recorders. If Sammy was out when something he wanted to watch was on TV, he recorded it for later viewing.

During shows, Mr. D sometimes told his audiences that he traveled with fifteen employees and a truck full of equipment. He joked that he was impressed with himself until he learned that Michael Jackson's entourage and cargo dwarfed his.

During the day, if not watching TV or a movie from his collection, Mr. D might read a mystery or play dominoes with Shirley or George. Other than for work, if he left his suite, it was to go out with friends for dinner, see a close friend perform, attend a fundraiser, or play golf. He was the first black man to host his own tournament—*The Sammy Davis Jr. Greater Hartford Open*, from 1974 to 1988. He golfed with a set of clubs given to him by Jerry Lewis.

Sammy stayed up late and slept until late in the morning. By noon, he was watching television. In every city, reporters anxiously awaited their interviews, but Sammy wouldn't meet with them until after his favorite soap operas, *All My Children* and *One Life to Live*.

To eat healthier and provide a constructive hobby, Sammy took up cooking in the late 1970s. On the road, he carried his own pots and pans and favorite staples like *Success Rice* and *Soup Starter* seasoning mix. A crew member would take his list to a grocery store for meat, seafood, and produce. For a time, Sammy had several of his own food products on the market, including his *Mean Mustard* and *Just Right Chili Seasoning*. Often, Mr. D would have a few of his entourage members in his suite for a meal or sample of his latest dish, usually members of A-Group and the stage crew. They spent the most time with Sammy.

Sammy found cooking therapeutic. In a 1982 documentary, he said it offered a mental break from his shows. "The only thing you think about is, I hope the sauce turns out."

CHAPTER 22

In June 1981, Sammy was scheduled for performances in London and Paris. Preceding that was a weekend at the Melody Fair Theater in North Tonawanda, NY. We stayed in nearby Buffalo. After opening night, I was back in my hotel room and couldn't sleep. I turned on the television, but there was nothing interesting to me, so I got dressed and went down to the lobby. They had a tastefully furnished reception area. I sat and people-watched, but there was little activity. Just as I was ready to return to my room, two Buffalo patrol officers walked in. Out of curiosity, I stayed to watch what they were doing. They just did a quick pass-through. I noticed they each carried smaller back-up guns in cross-draw holsters.

Damn, must be a rough town.

The next day, I joined the rest of the rhythm section and Fip Ricard for a half-hour drive to Niagara Falls. I had never seen the falls before. Before we boarded *Maid of the Mist*, the tour guide handed out thin ponchos for protection from the heavy mist. I learned there were actually three waterfalls along the border of New York State and Ontario, Canada. The tour included entry to one of the tunnels. The observation platform took us close to Horseshoe

Falls' raging water.

***

It was my first overseas trip. I arrived at London's Heathrow Airport and followed the signs to baggage claim. Halfway there, I spotted instrument cases and band equipment off to the side. They weren't Sammy's. There was a guy standing and leaning on a bass guitar case. He looked familiar.

Buddy Rich!

I walked over and introduced myself. He smiled and nodded in approval when I said I was Sammy's drummer. He shook my hand politely, though I could tell he wasn't in the mood to chat. I told him it was great to meet him, then moved on to claim my suitcases and catch a cab to our hotel.

***

London was Sammy's kind of town, and he had a long history of performing there. This time, his gig was for six nights at the Apollo Victoria Theater. It was part of a series of shows to raise money for Mr. D's *Freedom from Hunger Project,* which provided funding to aid agricultural development in third world countries.

During rehearsal, George called for a break. Off to the side stood a brunette—green dress, neat shoulder-length hair, maybe a few years older than me. She looked like she belonged there but also like she'd rather not be noticed. But she was very pretty, and naturally, I noticed.

"Hi, I'm Rick, Sammy's drummer."

"Hello, Rick, I'm Karen. I work in the theater office."

I was instantly captivated by Karen's big smile and satiny English accent. We chatted briefly, then returned to our jobs. After rehearsal, Dino started teasing me and saying he saw us smiling at each other. "Hey, P-Baby, now you gotta go to the office and bring her flowers," he said with an insistent tone. I laughed it off.

Sammy's opening act, *Wall Street Crash*, was a toe-tapping, finger-snapping septet—four guys and three gals—in white tie tuxedos with tails, swinging their tunes hard. My favorite was *It Don't Mean a Thing If It Ain't Got That Swing*.

After Sammy's opening night, I slept in as usual. After breakfast, I bought a bouquet of flowers, then headed to the theater. The whole way there, I wondered if Karen would be happy to see me or if I'd look like an idiot. When she saw the flowers, she beamed.

"Well, thank you, Rick," she said. "They're beautiful."

That accent!

That evening, Sammy performed his drum and voice medley again, loosely weaving seemingly unrelated songs. I was getting comfortable with the routine and took liberties to toss in appropriate accents and match his shifts in rhythm.

On our third night in London, Sammy invited the entourage and any guests to a screening of *An American Werewolf in London*. The horror flick had not yet been officially released. Mr. D, a longtime film buff, rented a theater for a private showing. It was a perfect opportunity, so I asked Karen to go with me, and she said yes. In the lobby, we got drinks and popcorn, courtesy of Sammy. It was odd being in a large theater with just twenty people taking their seats. There was a secluded spot I liked, but I wasn't sure Karen would agree. I pointed.

"How about that row there?" I asked her softly.

She smiled and nodded in approval.

The film opens with two young American men, David and Jack, arriving in England for a backpacking trip. Soon, the men hear distant howls of an unseen creature stalking them. Suddenly, the growling and ferocious werewolf attacked. Karen flinched and grabbed my arm, holding it tightly through the gory scene. When she finally loosened her grip, I put my arm around her.

I could feel a spark of attraction from her smiles and lingering glances. During a slow part of the movie, I turned to her, and we leaned in closer and kissed. Later, there was a steamy sex scene between one of the Americans and an older English nurse. I sat motionless, hoping Karen wasn't uncomfortable and that the scene would end quickly. After the movie, Karen told me she'd see me at the Apollo Victoria Theater before Sammy's next show. We kissed again, said goodbye, and went our separate ways.

It was an exciting time to be in London with the royal wedding of Prince Charles and Lady Diana Spencer approaching. Newspapers, magazines, and shops were filled with commemorative items. As a belated birthday gift for my sister Susan, I purchased an oversized Wedgewood mug—white with platinum and dark blue accents and featuring silhouettes of the soon-to-be royal bride and groom.

If it hadn't been for Fip, Mickey, Frank, and Gary, I would have missed out on many of the sights I saw. At eighteen, it never occurred to me to take advantage of my off time in cities I might never visit again. Sammy's other musicians never made that mistake. We spent an afternoon visiting London's historic attractions, like Big Ben at the Houses of Parliament. As we walked, I spotted a bobby. The police officer agreed to pose with me, and Gary snapped a photo. At Buckingham Palace, we attended the changing of the Queen's Guard. Later, we enjoyed dinner at an Indian restaurant.

The next evening after the show, I invited Karen to a late dinner at a lively Greek eatery. Opa! Afterward, we walked back to my hotel. This time, we didn't go our separate ways. We enjoyed time together for two more nights. After Sammy's closing show, there were no tears or sad goodbyes. I felt like we understood our time together was going to be brief.

"Maybe we'll see each other again if Sammy returns to London," Karen said.

"I hope so."

The next morning, I packed my luggage and called for a porter. I grabbed my passport, about twenty pounds, and my small folding knife, slipping them into my pocket. A few minutes later, the porter arrived to bring my two suitcases out to our transportation. I tipped him and then headed for the elevator. At the front desk, I paid my incidentals and turned in my key, then joined our entourage members in the van.

At Heathrow, several of us checked in to get our boarding passes. I was last in line at the security checkpoint. The metal detector started beeping. I knew it was my little knife. When I pulled it out, the security attendant waved to someone. It never dawned on me that my pocketknife might get me arrested and thrown into a London jail. But that's what I was thinking when I saw two police officers walking toward me. One of them was toting a small machine gun over his shoulder. Both were expressionless as they eyeballed me. I looked for the guys, but they were up ahead, walking toward the gate.

Oh shit. I'm in trouble.

Despite their deadpan stares, the officers were friendly. They explained that I couldn't bring my knife onboard and would have to check it. One of them gave me a large padded envelope and directed me to write my name on it, then took it away. They did not take me away. Relieved, I walked quickly to catch up to the rest of the musicians. When I told them what had happened, they just laughed. I soon learned that the rise in airplane hijackings in the late 1960s had led to stricter airport security, particularly in Europe.

We were off on our first day in Paris. I stepped outside the Hilton International looking for breakfast and spotted a bakery—perfect. I grabbed a croissant and chocolate milk and sat at an outdoor table. For a moment, my mind drifted back to Karen. We'd only spent a few days together. It wasn't love, but it was something special. I wished we'd had more time. The sound of traffic pulled me back to the street. It all felt surreal.

I'm in Paris playing drums for Sammy Davis, Jr.

Sammy was performing at the Lido Theater, delivering a tribute to the legendary Maurice Chevalier, a master of French music and comedy. After rehearsal, George introduced me to Michael Silva, Mr. D's first drummer, who came to visit Sammy and George. When Michael left Sammy, he settled in Paris.

Sammy's show opened with a troupe of about two dozen dancers—mostly young women. I was milling around backstage when they headed out for their opener. They were topless. I was staring at the walls but could tell through my peripheral vision. For their second song, they returned in full regalia—feathers, sequins, and sky-high headpieces, all in bold colors.

Sammy's show went much as usual, though he included his voice and drum medley. And it was the first time I heard him impersonate Maurice Chevalier during a theatrical and comedic chorus of *Me and My Shadow*.

The next day, I met up with the rest of Sammy's musicians for dinner at a café. We chatted as usual. It was seldom about music. We often spoke about Sammy's current engagement and the city we were in, and we laughed about the latest rumors going around B-Group. Often our conversations veered into eclectic topics. I listened as Fip, Mickey, Frank, and Gary debated how to pronounce "sorbet," a cold treat, much like sherbet. Then came world history and nuclear war.

"I'd want to be at ground zero," Frank said.

One of the guys nodded in agreement.

I chimed in, "I'd want to be as far away as possible."

The following afternoon we took a cab ride to walk around the Eiffel Tower. I brought my camera and took pictures, including a shot of two Parisian police officers on foot patrol.

CHAPTER 23

After Paris, it was back home. Sammy went to Nashville to record an album called *The Closest of Friends*. I was disappointed to learn he was using local musicians. A few days later, we were back at Lake Tahoe. Mr. D had a two-week gig at Harrah's Headliner Room. His opening act was Byron Allen, a twenty-year-old comedian and co-host of the TV show *Real People*. Byron and Dino became friends. One night, they met three young, pretty women. The guys were interested in two of the girls and invited them out. The two girls did not want to leave their friend behind, so Dino and Byron recruited me as a backup. It was my first triple date. My evening soured when I tried to put my arm around my date, but she leaned away.

***

South Lake Tahoe, California, was a second home for Sammy and his entourage. Right on the border of Stateline, Nevada, the region combined the glitter of Las Vegas with the beauty of snow-capped mountains, ski resorts like Heavenly Valley and Squaw Valley (they've since been renamed), and Lake Tahoe's calm blue

water. Breathtaking Emerald Bay was said to be one of the most photographed natural settings in the world. For a kid from Cleveland,
this was like stepping into a postcard. In contrast to Las Vegas, the
hotels and casinos mirrored the region's mellower vibe.

The excitement of performing at Harrah's at Lake Tahoe peaked
after arriving at the Reno airport. We took a shuttle van for the
hour-and-fifteen-minute drive up along the Sierra Nevada mountain
range, past Carson City, and into South Lake Tahoe. Lake Tahoe
sits over 6,000 feet up. Thinner air, less oxygen—they said—but I
never really noticed it.

Occasionally, Sammy flew directly into Lake Tahoe's small airport. He performed so often at Lake Tahoe that several Harrah's
employees became close friends with B-Group. In particular, there
were two young women who were blackjack dealers. They became
pals with our stage crew members and hosted a barbecue party for
the entourage during the summers.

***

Because of my interest in police work, I gravitated toward
Sammy's security officers. As a result, Mickey took to calling me
Ranger Rick. If things were quiet at Harrah's, I would chat with the
officer stationed outside Mr. D's dressing room. One of them, Dick
Conway, a former deputy sheriff, was about forty-five years old. He
and I became friends. During the shows, Dick was stationed on
stage right while bodyguard DuWayne Rice roamed stage left. After
shows, if Sammy was leaving quickly, Dick accompanied him and
Altovise out of the dressing room area. The dressing room for Mr.
D's musicians was at the end of the hallway adjacent to Harrah's
main kitchen. Sammy and Altovise usually peeked in to say goodnight before heading through the kitchen to avoid the crowds and
take the back way up to Mr. D's suite. Often, they'd ride a golf cart
with Mr. D at the wheel.

After work, Dick and I sometimes joined a small group for bowling and breakfast. Other times, we'd sit in Harrah's coffee shop, playing Keno, a lottery-type game where you select numbers and a runner takes bets to the Keno parlor. Drawings were held every twenty minutes. Remote video monitors throughout the casino and restaurants allowed bettors to view the winning numbers. One night, I won a thousand dollars. We tipped our runner well, but Dick had to collect the winnings since I was only nineteen and couldn't gamble. I tried to give him a hundred dollars, but he wouldn't take it.

Dick knew I was interested in police work. He told me stories about incidents he handled at Harrah's, like a horrible accident in the kitchen. Dick was the first security officer on the scene after a young worker, trying to clear a jam in the industrial garbage disposal, bypassed the safety mechanism and reached in just as the unit started. He moaned in pain, blood pouring from his mangled hand. Dick applied a tourniquet. The victim survived but lost his hand. One evening, while Sammy was performing, a gunman robbed the casino cashier's cage, firing a shot into the floor before fleeing. After the show, Dick showed me the hole in the carpet. He told me Nevada took casino crimes very seriously and that the guy would surely get caught and go to prison for a long time.

On another evening, between Sammy's shows, a new eighteen-year-old hotel employee entered the backstage area near the dressing rooms. He wanted Mr. D's autograph. It was a serious violation, and management fired him. The next morning, Dick picked me up to go horseback riding. As we drove on the main road, he pointed out a pedestrian, a young man with a backpack, heading out of town. It was the kid who'd been fired. I couldn't help but wonder if he was homeless—where he would go or what he would do next.

***

I shouldn't have been gambling or hanging out in the lounges. But once in a while, like when I was with my brother in Las Vegas, I played the poker slots. I only gambled when a member of Sammy's entourage was nearby. It was a good thing because one time, my machine started dinging loudly. Heads turned in my direction. Shirley Rhodes came over and claimed my machine before an employee arrived. She collected the $1100 win and tipped the casino employee $100 for me. When the employee left, I insisted that Shirley take $100, but she was having none of it.

The entertainment scene in Nevada's cabaret rooms and lounges was top notch, featuring acts like *Paul Revere and the Raiders*, the *Coasters,* and BB King. After one of Sammy's shows at Harrah's in Reno, stage crewman Lester Mornay and I were enjoying the Dae Han Sisters. They were a high-energy Korean family, originally known as the Seoul Sisters, who played a mix of top forty hits and originals. Lester and I traded opinions about which one was most attractive. The one who caught our attention had a constant, contagious smile. She moved frenetically to the rhythm, frequently toweling sweat from her face.

Like in Las Vegas, Lake Tahoe offered the comfort of familiar faces for Sammy, including close friends Doug Bushhousen and Holmes Hendricksen, Harrah's entertainment directors. I learned that years earlier, Holmes, the VP of entertainment, had promised Sammy that no headliner would earn more than him. The house orchestra knew Sammy's arrangements well, and crew members were familiar with the stage set-up and routine. It was a fun working environment, and Mr. D was always in top form at "The Lake."

***

Sammy's musicians and crew stayed at the Royal Valhalla Motel. With stunning views of Lake Tahoe and a friendly staff, the Royal Val was a favorite for B-Group. The queen beds made my single-sized bed at home seem like a cot. Our rooms even had small kitchens. Several of us took advantage of these efficiency suites to get away from restaurant food. We shopped at Raley's grocery store and had fun cooking. Fip Ricard was an old hand at soul food. I was new in the kitchen but enjoyed trying to duplicate my maternal grandmother's Italian recipes. I once made stuffed calamari, carefully spooning a breadcrumb, garlic, and parsley mixture into squid tubes and securing them with toothpicks. For dessert, I made cannoli. I fashioned the tubes for the pastry shells from rolled-up aluminum foil. I might even slow-cook a pot of tomato sauce flavored with some ground beef and pork or meatballs and sausage.

When it was time for work, we often made the short walk to Harrah's. Even in winter, some of us skipped the taxi so we could pass under snow-frosted pines and catch the cheery scent of wood burning in fireplaces—some from tiny houses, others from old motel lobbies. After fifteen minutes, the view suddenly opened up to busy Route 50 and the front of Harrah's.

Sammy's one- or two-week gigs—like those at Harrah's Lake Tahoe, Harrah's Reno, or Caesars Palace in Vegas—were more relaxed than his weekend engagements. The stage crews in the Nevada showrooms felt like an extension of Sammy's own team. Sometimes, Mr. D would play movie trivia with them as he passed through.

Five minutes before showtime, the musicians settled in, opened their charts, tuned up softly, and chatted in low tones. Then we turned our attention to George Rhodes, nattily dressed in a suit and tie, as he made his way onto the stage, eased up to the podium and casually greeted the band.

"Can't get out of it now," he might joke.

In the background, we'd hear a house stagehand shout in his Hispanic accent, "Fire curtain going up!" This was our signal to quiet down, as the thick fire curtain was being raised—just one minute before showtime. From that point, only the regular curtain would separate us from the audience. When George was ready to begin, he gave Mickey Laverine an "Okay, hit it" to play the lead-in piano notes to *Murphy Here.*

Mr. D often mentioned his penchant for jewelry—bracelets, rings, necklaces, and pendants. My favorite was the lapel pin he often wore—a diamond-crusted "S" in a triangular frame—the unmistakable *Superman* logo. He wore jewelry offstage as well, though he reserved his most extravagant pieces for performances. He explained that he wore so much jewelry because it was theatrical.

"It's bigger than life," he'd say. "It's pizzazz, and it don't hurt nobody."

Then, he would take the opportunity for some laughs.

"But I don't wear my jewelry when I'm out on the street. In fact I don't know any street I can walk down wearin' all this stuff. They might be waiting for me around the corner."

The audience laughs, and Sammy switches to a street-corner accent:

"Here he comes. Get him!"

He switches back.

"And that's just in the white neighborhoods."

Sammy's fondness for jewelry was good fodder for journalists and comedians, like Milton Berle, who joked that Sammy was the only man he knew who showered with a metal detector. After the first few tunes, Sammy would remove some of his rings and place them in the piano well. "Keep an eye on those," he might instruct Mickey Laverine. Then he would scoot over to George and, in mock secrecy, whisper, "George, keep an eye on Mickey." The audience laughed. I did, too.

***

We were back at Harrah's in Reno, and the show had just started.

As usual, I was feeling warm. I looked down and realized I forgot to turn my fan on. Sammy had finished his first three songs and was monologuing. I reached down and flipped the power switch. It caused a POP! in my monitor.

Mental note. Don't do that again.

A few heads in the band turned in my direction, but I played innocent. That's when I noticed her. She was a violinist and appeared to be in her twenties with jet-black hair and an exotic bi-racial look. After several days, I asked the house percussionist about her. Her name was Gina. Before I knew it, it was closing night. We'd be leaving in the morning. As usual, Sammy was ending his show with *Mr. Bojangles*. But first, derby in hand, he bid the audience goodbye. Sammy joked about Harrah's entertainment directors discussing his return. "I think I'll be back around January," he said. "I tell you this because I overheard Holmes Hendricksen tell Doug Bushhousen, 'It will be a cold day when Sammy's back.' So I figured that's January or maybe February."

After the laughs, Sammy explained how *Mr. Bojangles* was special to him. The three-quarter-time tune was written in the 1960s by Jerry Jeff Walker, a country and folk singer. Sammy adopted it and released it on a 1972 album. The title came from the name of the great tap dancer and actor Bill "Bojangles" Robinson, who was active during the first half of the nineteen hundreds. The lyrics have nothing to do with Robinson's life. Instead, they tell the story of an aging hoofer jailed for excessive drinking, struggling to make a living as a traveling dancer. Mr. D sometimes told his audience that he feared becoming like Mr. Bojangles.

I had my brushes ready as Sammy kicked off the rhythm section: "Oon chink a-chinka, oon chink a-chinka," and we were into a vamp led by Frank Accardo's crisp guitar figure. Sammy whistled his usual eight-bar solo, then started singing. *Mr. Bojangles* was one of Sammy's more theatrical numbers—pensive lyrics combined with a dramatic delivery, polished to perfection and wedded with graceful dance moves. The string section breezed in, and I switched to sticks. The arrangement heated as Sammy sang:

"Mr. Bojangles, come back and dance. Dance. Dance."

Toward the end of the song, Sammy removed his hat. The strings faded out, I went back to brushes, and we returned to the rhythm section vamp. The stage was dark—just a lone spotlight on Mr. D. With one knee cocked, he took his familiar closing stance, the same one on his music stands. With the spotlight dimming, he donned his derby again and whistled the final eight bars.

He lifted his hand in the air and gazed upward as if to say, "I have conquered my fear."

As George cut off the last note, Sammy's spotlight went dark. And as always, the applause ramped up quickly. I grabbed my sticks, and George gave the downbeat for the bows—a closing song always played while Sammy took his final bows.

In his signature farewell, he raised his right hand—peace sign to fist—and bid, "Peace, love, and togetherness."

I started packing my drums quickly, eager to hopefully meet Gina before we left. For Sammy's engagements that lasted a week or longer, he held an opening night party and a closing night party for the house band and stage crew. It would be a perfect opportunity to meet Gina, assuming she attended. Jolly Brown and Lester Mornay were nearby, collecting Sammy's music books and starting to break down the stands. I glanced over at the party area. Sammy was smiling and joking with the musicians. I tried to spot Gina when I slipped off the riser.

As I caught myself, Jolly let out a belly laugh. "What, Sticks? You got a hot date?"

Lester chimed in, "If you got a date, brother, you better slow down and get there in one piece."

They laughed and I finished packing in twenty minutes. My

shirt was wet with sweat when I walked over to the tables. The buffet featured Chinese appetizers, shrimp cocktails, and bottles of Pouilly-Fuissé wine. I didn't see Gina, so I grabbed a plate and put three crab claws and an eggroll on it. While eating, I chatted with a couple of the house musicians. I was disappointed when I spotted Gina. She had her violin case and was walking toward the exit. I headed in that direction as if leaving and intercepted her.

"Hi."

"Well, good job there, fella."

"I'm Rick."

"I know," she chuckled. "I've been paying attention."

I smiled. There was an uncomfortable pause as I waited for her to tell me her name. I didn't want her to know that I already knew it. Just as she said, "I'm Gina," a cellist approached with her case, pausing as it became clear they were leaving together.

"Nice meeting you, Gina."

She and her friend turned to leave. "Bye."

CHAPTER 24

In August 1981, Sammy returned to Caesars Palace in Las Vegas. The temperature hit the mid-nineties, and the sun blasted the desert. It was the first time I heard, "But it's a dry heat." I chuckled. Sure, Vegas lacked the humidity of the Midwest, but stepping outside felt like sticking my head into a 350-degree oven.

B-Group was back at the Ambassador Inn. That's where I met Sherry, a cashier in the "cage" where gamblers exchanged coins and chips. She was clearly older than me, but her flashy blue eyes, red hair, petite frame, and playful grin caught my attention—and she knew it. She held my gaze a beat longer than necessary with a little half-smile like we were onto something no one else could see.

***

One night during the run at Caesars, Sammy demonstrated his skill with a Colt Western-style revolver, a routine from earlier years. It was the only time I saw him break out his custom-made belt and holster. He drew his six-gun, twirled it in different directions, and re-holstered it with blazing speed. I flinched, as did some in the audience when he fired a deafening blank into the air for the grand finale.

During Sammy's two-week engagement, I spent a lot of time with my brother and my cousins. After Las Vegas, we were off to New England, where Mr. D had a weekend engagement at his longtime friend Buster Bonoff's Warwick Musical Theater in Providence, Rhode Island. The Warwick was one of the nation's relatively few theaters in the round. The design harks back to ancient Greece and has the audience surrounding the stage. Others included Valley Forge Music Fair in Philadelphia, Pine Knob in Detroit, and the Front Row back home.

On these rotating stages, Sammy joked that he felt like he was in a rotisserie. "You can take me out now," he'd shout, "I'm brown all over."

From Providence, we moved on to the South Shore Music Circus in Cohasset, Massachusetts. Opening for Mr. D was soul organist and singer Billy Preston. He had several hits, including *Nothing from Nothing* and *Will It Go Round in Circles,* and one of my favorites, *That's the Way God Planned It.* In Providence, our hotel restaurant had a whole lobster dinner special. It included corn on the cob, a baked potato, and a salad for $6.95. Many of us had lobster for dinner every night.

***

In September 1981, Sammy was a guest on the Jerry Lewis Muscular Dystrophy Association Labor Day Telethon. The iconic weekend, with its eclectic mix of entertainers, was a TV tradition for my family. At the time, we were in the middle of a one-week engagement at Caesars Boardwalk Regency Cabaret Theater in Atlantic City. Sammy's appearance was broadcast remotely.

Jerry Lewis introduced Sammy on a split screen. Mr. D encouraged donations and mentioned that his crew had contributed $1,000, though we were never asked to chip in; it was all his money. After one song by Mr. D, the two pals bantered back and forth with their signature silliness. Sammy scatted a fast-paced jazz tune and challenged Jerry to follow.

Jerry, feigning alarm, said, "Hold it, Sammy, I'm white!"—which got a big laugh.

Meanwhile, my parents were thrilled to see me on TV with Sammy.

Later that month, Sammy performed at the grand opening of the Gerald R. Ford Presidential Museum in Grand Rapids, Michigan. The all-star gala was held at the 2500-seat Grand Rapids Convention Center. Celebrating with former President Ford and his wife Betty were President and Mrs. Reagan, Vice President George H.W. Bush, House Speaker Tip O'Neill, Canadian Prime Minister Pierre Trudeau, Mexican President Jose Lopez Portillo, and many other government dignitaries.

Sammy's musicians would only be playing two tunes with him. It was the first time without my own drum set. George knew I wasn't happy but dismissed my worries. "You just do the best you can under the worst circumstances." The bright side was that the house drummer was right-handed. It seemed that ninety percent of drummers played right-handed. For the first time, I was grateful that, as a southpaw, I'd been taught to play right-handed. Before rehearsal began, I made peace with the house drummer's rather small kit without making any adjustments.

In the early evening, we returned to the convention center. As I was walking with a group of Sammy's entourage toward the doors, I was pleasantly surprised to see Pearl Bailey and Louie Bellson. I didn't know they were on the show. Louie greeted me with a big smile and hug.

When we reached the stage entrance, I opened the door for Pearl. She paused and looked at me. "You're only holding the door for me because I said some nice things to you at Louie's drum contest."

She had a straight face, but I could tell she was joking. I didn't know what to say. I just smiled. Besides Pearl Bailey and Sammy, the bill included Bob Hope, Danny Thomas, Tony Orlando, Glen Campbell, and the U.S. Air Force Presidential Drill Team. The event was so big that I didn't see Louie and Pearl again that night.

As the show got underway, I found myself getting restless, as I often did during long waits in the dressing room or the green room where musicians prepared to go on. I wandered off, chatting with a nearby police officer or just seeing what else was happening backstage. I left Frank, Gary, Fip, and Mickey behind and stepped out of the brightly lit green room. I found myself in a dimly lit backstage corridor, where I noticed an older man in a tuxedo studying a piece of paper.

Damn. It's Bob Hope!

I knew Bob Hope was from Cleveland and that my maternal grandfather had gone to school with him. Surely the comedian would like to hear that and meet me. I approached with a smile.

"Excuse me, Mr. Hope, I'm Sammy's drum—"

"Can't you see I'm rehearsing!"

"Oh, excuse me." I turned to escape my professional blunder while muttering to myself.

Asshole.

Back in the green room, there was more to hold my attention—specifically, Tony Orlando's foxy backup singers, Dawn: Joyce Vincent Wilson and Telma Hopkins. I tried not to gawk.

Tony sang a lot of light, upbeat pop tunes. The ones I knew best were *Tie a Yellow Ribbon Round the Ole Oak Tree* and *Say, Has Anybody Seen My Sweet Gypsy Rose,* songs I occasionally played, as instrumental versions, in small groups around Cleveland. Tony was nowhere in sight. None of the stars were. I figured they had their own green room.

After about forty-five minutes of waiting, the other musicians and I were summoned to the stage. We slipped into place. Mr. D appeared above the band on a multi-tiered staircase, wearing a tux with an open collar and a cravat tie held by a pendant ring. George looked up and gave a nod to Mickey, who hit the keynote for the piano and vocal intro to *The Birth of the Blues*. Sammy started singing:

"Oh, they say my people long ago,
Were looking for a different tune,
One that we could croon,
As only we can..."

I glanced past George toward the audience. President Reagan and former President Ford sat side by side in a mezzanine box, flanked by their wives. They smiled as Sammy slowly made his way down the stairs and, over Mickey's fat, bluesy fills, finished the intro:

"...This is how the blues began..."

Sammy paused, then hit his three pickup notes—"We heard the..."—and launched into the melody as George's baton dropped, perfectly in sync, as usual, with Mr. D's timing.

"...Breeze,
through the trees,
Singin' weird melodies,
And we named it,
the start of the blues..."

As the foot-stomping arrangement kicked in, Mr. D got the audience clapping—including Presidents Reagan and Ford. The drum set didn't have any large crash cymbals, so I played harder than usual to fill out the sound.

"...From a whippoorwill,
high on a hill,
We took a new note,
Pushed it through a horn,

Until it was worn,
Into a new note.
Get it, get it!
We nursed it,
And we rehearsed it,
Then they gave out the news,
That the South land,
Gave birth to the blues."

Near the end, Sammy turned and directed the final three chords himself. He bowed to generous applause and nodded to the presidential box. He usually reprised *Birth of the Blues*, so I stayed ready. Sure enough, he turned to the band and shouted, "One more time!" and started singing:

"From a whippoorwill..."

Later in the show, Foster Brooks performed. The white-haired, bearded comedian's act consisted entirely—and to perfection—of impersonating a drunk. It was hilarious to watch Presidents Reagan and Ford, dignified current and former Commanders-in-Chief, laughing and shaking their heads in amusement as Foster swayed, slurred, stuttered, and belched through mispronounced words. The fun started the moment he was introduced:

"You're probably wondering why I'm a-p-p-pearing in this condition. I have a good reason. And if you giiiive me a moment, I'll explain. (Pause.) I've been drinking all day."

After the show, when I returned to my hotel room, I reconsidered my judgment of Bob Hope. When I approached him to mention my grandfather, I didn't know he was the event's master of ceremonies. At seventy-eight, he was understandably busy. A lesson learned.

***

In October 1981, Sammy received an honorary doctorate in literature from Atlanta University. Afterward, his itinerary changed unexpectedly. The entourage joined him in Las Vegas, where he subbed for Tom Jones, whose father had died in Wales.

Sammy's special guest was "Count" Basie and his orchestra. Mr. D's relationship with Bill Basie dated back to the early days of the Will Mastin Trio, and they later recorded an album together. It was a special engagement for me. I'd revered the Count Basie band since I was a boy, practicing along to their albums in our drum room. With my brother having worked for them and the band even coming to our house for dinner, I felt a personal connection. Several of the musicians asked about Ray. Some recalled being at our home.

An hour before showtime on the second night, I introduced myself to Count Basie, who was seventy-seven and used a motorized scooter. He graciously posed for a photo with me. During the engagement, I spoke with longtime Basie trombonist Bill Hughes. He asked if I was saving money and advised me on personal finance, encouraging me to consider investing in real estate.

After Vegas, Sammy's next gig was a tribute to Senator Barry Goldwater in Tucson. Prior to that, I had several days off at home. I ran my usual errands and ordered a book that Bill Hughes recommended on investing. The day before my flight to Arizona, I was watching the news on television. There had been a shootout at a bank robbery. A Cleveland police officer was killed. Saddened and angered, I felt a grim sense of satisfaction knowing the officer had seriously wounded his assailant.

The Barry Goldwater tribute dinner in Tucson also raised funds for a mental health clinic and alcohol treatment center. Former First Lady Betty Ford was a guest. She spoke openly about her battle with alcoholism. Before Sammy's performance, President Reagan appeared via remote on a big screen. The following day, we returned to Las Vegas.

Around this time, Brian Dellow replaced DuWayne Rice as Mr. D's chief security officer. Tall and professional, he often wore a suit or sport coat. He was from England and had served as a military police officer and intelligence agent. Brian had done previous security work for Sammy but would now travel with him full-time.

In Las Vegas, B-Group returned to the off-Strip Ambassador Inn, where I struck up a connection with Sherry, the blue-eyed, red-haired cashier with a few years on me. Like several of the other employees, she got friendly with me and the other guys. When she took her break or the casino was slow, we'd have long chats. Sherry was wound a little tight, maybe stressed with life, but would light up a cigarette and start to relax. She talked lovingly about her four-year-old daughter, her mom, and her two cats. Sherry laughed at herself as she vented about people who annoyed her—mostly her ex-husband and one of the other girls she worked with. I told her about traveling with Sammy, hanging out with my brother in Vegas, and my interest in police work.

One afternoon, Sherry joined me at the Ambassador Inn coffee shop. Her bright blue eyes drew me in as Jimmy Buffett's *Margaritaville* played overhead.

"I love your eyes," I blurted out.

"You young flirt," she said, reaching for a cigarette. I grabbed her lighter and clicked it on. She held my hand, lit up, and then asked how old I was.

"Nineteen."

"God, fourteen years younger than me," she said, shaking her head. "Well, you know what they say."

"No, what?"

Sherry took a long drag off her cigarette and exhaled to the side, the smoke trailing off before she spoke.

"Age is just mind over matter," she said with a little smirk.

"Yeah?"

"Yeah. If you don't mind, it doesn't matter."

We laughed. Our attraction was intense despite our age difference—or maybe because of it.

I invited Sherry to Sammy's show, and Brian Dellow let her sit on stage right. Afterward, Sherry and I climbed into her old Toyota, originally silver but faded dull gray by the Las Vegas sun. We pulled out of the rear lot and passed the front of Caesars, its lights shimmering in the fountain streams, even more spectacular at night.

At the Ambassador Inn, Sherry grabbed a heavy tote bag from the back seat, and we headed toward my room.

"What do you have, a gun in there?" I asked.

"Never you mind."

I closed the door behind us.

"Get your bathing suit on," Sherry said, her tone playful yet commanding.

"As you wish." She disappeared into the bathroom with her bag still in hand.

Two minutes later, she emerged, tossing me a towel. She had put her red locks up and was wearing a bikini. I grinned, bit my lip, and gave her a once-over.

"Ouch!" I said.

Sherry chuckled. "Flattery will get you everywhere."

She reached into her bag and pulled out a bottle of wine and two plastic cups, then her eyes landed on my chest.

"Now, what happened there?" she asked, inspecting the scar and pushing one area with her index finger.

"How'd ya burn yourself?"

"Hot coffee when I was a kid."

"Ouch," she said with a grimace. "Well, bad-ass scar anyway, drummer boy."

I smiled.

"C'mon," she said, heading for the door.

I followed Sherry toward the courtyard. It was nearly 1:00 a.m., and the pool had been closed since 11:00. The lights were off, so I was surprised when she pulled on the gate—and it opened.

"I'm friends with the security guard," she said with a smirk. "But we've got to be quiet."

Sherry nodded toward the motel rooms behind us, all with the drapes drawn. We slipped into the steaming jacuzzi. I took a seat across from her. She shot me a look that said, "Get over here," and motioned with her hand. I slid over and snuggled in next to Sherry as the heat wrapped around us like a blanket.

"Now you're talking," she said with a grin. "It's been a while since I soaked next to a shirtless drummer with no lifeguard in sight."

We laughed loud enough to catch ourselves. Sherry poured us glasses of wine and for about forty-five minutes, we sipped, chatted in hushed voices and laughed softly as we looked up at the desert stars—and at each other. I had my arm around her. She turned to face me and kissed me, softly at first, then firmer as I pressed in.

"Enough fun," she said, standing to slip out of the water.

We toweled off and walked back to my room, the buzz of wine and steam still between us. Just before I unlocked the door, Sherry gave me a sly, knowing smile.

***

Though my confidence had grown after nine months with Sammy's show, there were still moments when self-doubt crept in. A-Group and B-Group were staying at the same hotel when George Rhodes handed me a box from Sammy. He said it was a gift. Inside was a metronome. I immediately assumed it was a hint about my timing—a crucial skill for any drummer. Though many musicians used metronomes for practice, I couldn't shake the feeling that Sammy was trying to tell me something. I stewed about it for the rest of the evening.

The next day, I mentioned my concern to George before the show. He burst out laughing.

"Ricky, you got the job. What are you worried about? Sammy just thought it would be a nice gift for his drummer."

"I guess I overthought it," I said, embarrassed.

A few days later, Ray called me to catch up. I told him about my reaction to Mr. D giving me a metronome, and we both laughed. He told me how Sammy sometimes played the drums during the show.

"For a while, he carried his own drum set," he said. "Actually, I think he borrowed them from Louie Bellson."

"I never saw them."

"He stopped doing it a couple of years before I left," Ray explained. "The drums were set up on a portable riser, and if Sammy wanted, the crew rolled it onto the stage."

"A few weeks ago, Mr. D came up and took over my drums," I told Ray.

He played *How High the Moon* just with Fip and the rhythm section, right?

"Yeah."

There was a pause and Ray chuckled.

"That reminds me," he said. "One time, Sammy came up to play my set. Before I stepped off the drum riser, I grabbed all my sticks and took them with me. Sammy was looking around for sticks, and everyone in the band cracked up."

"Oh, that's funny," I said. "So what did Sammy do?"

"He played along like he was mad and yelled, 'Ray, bring those sticks back here!' The audience was laughing, too."

It was a typical exchange between me and Ray—funny stories, jokes, humorous observations—whatever made us laugh.

Me with Michael Silva, Sammy Davis, Jr.'s first drummer.
Paris, 1981.

Wall Street Crash, a swingin' and dynamic UK act, opened for
Sammy at London's Apollo Victoria Theatre in 1981. L–R: Jean
Rich, Peter Olsen, James Graeme, Paul Felber, Mary Dunne,
Colin Copperfield, and Siobhan McCarthy. Their music director
was Keith Strachan.

Sammy and singer Tony Orlando greet President Ronald Reagan during dedication ceremonies for the Gerald R. Ford Presidential Museum in Grand Rapids, Michigan, September 1981. In the background, comedian Foster Brooks greets a partially visible First Lady Nancy Reagan.

Courtesy Ronald Reagan Presidential Library.

Former President Ford waves to applause while President Reagan, First Lady Reagan, and former First Lady Ford look on from their box at the DeVos Place Convention Center in Grand Rapids, Michigan, September 1981.

Courtesy Ronald Reagan Presidential Library.

CHAPTER 25

When the curtain rose and the overture finished, Sammy almost always made his entrance with music. It might be a short and repetitive "play-on" piece or the intro to his first tune. But sometimes, he'd surprise the crowd by stepping onto the stage in silence, bathed in a single spotlight.

As the applause died down, he'd introduce himself. "Hello, I'm Sammy Davis, Jr."

The line was pointless, but it never failed to get a chuckle from the crowd. "No, I take no chances," he might explain with mock sincerity. "I let you know who I am right from the start. It eliminates a lot of chatter in case somebody doesn't recognize me."

Sammy's shows, I would come to realize, were largely retrospectives of his life. He spoke between songs as if the audience was sitting in his living room. There were brief accounts of his youthful days with his dad and uncle, his rise to success, and his friendship with Frank Sinatra. He compared himself to youthful entertainers.

If there was a celebrity in the audience, Sammy graciously acknowledged him or her. Once, he introduced famed pro footballer Rosey Grier, a six-and-a-half-footer weighing nearly three hundred pounds. When the applause stopped, Sammy asked Rosey if he could have one of his old ties.

"I'd like to use it," Mr. D explained, "to make a suit."

There were plenty of other moments of silliness. It might be racial or self-deprecating humor, but it was always void of profanity.

One time, when his joke bombed, Sammy flipped a stereotype in retaliation. "I'll move into your neighborhood," he said, pausing dramatically as Mickey launched into *On the Street Where You Live*. "And bring up your property values."

Sometimes, Sammy used Mickey, who was white, as a foil. "Why don't you play on some of the black keys?" Or he might complain to George, "I told you we should've hired a black piano player." The audience loved it.

Sammy was a mimic of dozens of voices. For example, he'd don a German accent to introduce music from the play *Faust* by Johann Wolfgang von Goethe. "Next, ladies and gentlemen, I would like to sing *Faust*. Then I will sing slow. And then I will sing *Faust* again."

Sammy would suddenly recite a line from an old movie or break into an impromptu impersonation. Occasionally, it was of Vaudevillian comedian W.C. Fields crankily shooing away an annoying child. I'd crack a rim shot for each sidekick of Mr. D's foot. "Get away, kid. You draw flies."

Sammy often broke into his British voice, exaggerating his rolled Rs as he recited lines from Shakespeare. I marveled at how effortlessly he memorized the lines. Every now and then, he'd have Neil Shurmer play an audio recording from *The Music Man*, the musical about a con man named Harold Hill who visits a small town and promises to organize a youth band to keep the boys in line. Sammy would lip sync perfectly to Hill's lively and catchy, *Ya Got Trouble*.

When Sammy sang a ballad with just the rhythm section, he'd send George offstage.

"Go have a smoke, George. Just make sure it has a name on it."

Sammy smoked often, especially onstage. A typical show might see him burn through three or four Pall Malls. It was part of the swingin' cool Rat Pack image—cigarette in one hand, cocktail in the other. Sometimes, he'd express regret over smoking, calling it his only remaining vice. He'd discourage young people from smoking.

"I'm not proud of it—it's a filthy habit."

Then he'd segue into a chorus of *Smoke! Smoke! Smoke!*, a Western novelty tune—more narrated than sung—about a smoker arriving at heaven's gates and asking St. Peter to wait while he has one last cigarette.

Sammy loved country and Western music. We had been doing a Kenny Rogers medley of about eight tunes, including *She Believes in Me*, *You Decorated My Life*, and *Lucille*. Sammy would joke about his white audience not clapping. "This is your music!" After the laughs, he'd get them singing along to *The Gambler*. The medley featured toe-tapping guitar solos, and Sammy always gave the nod to Frank Accardo's "pickin' and clickin'."

Around this time, Mr. D added a medley from *Stop the World: I Want to Get Off*. I recalled the title from my brother playing drums in Sammy's Broadway production. It was co-written by Londoners Anthony Newley and Leslie Bricusse, longtime friends of Mr. D and the source of some of his music, including one of his hits, *What Kind of Fool Am I*. Sammy introduced the medley as a "capsule version" of the play—the tale of a commoner named Little Chap (played by Sammy) and his roller-coaster search for happiness, romance, wealth, and the meaning of life. The songs included *Someone Nice Like You*, *Once in a Lifetime*, *I Wanna Be Rich*, and *Gonna Build a Mountain*.

Sammy usually performed one tap dance number during his shows. He would often reach into the piano well to bring out his black patent leather tap shoes. The sight of the shiny silver plates on the heels and toes, followed by the sharp CLACK when he intentionally dropped them to the floor, always prompted eager applause.

He'd reach into the piano again. This time, he would bring out his prized gold-colored and tasseled three-foot-long shoehorn from England, custom-made from the sword of a Queen's Guard member.

Applause would transition to scattered laughter as Sammy stood there, working the shoehorn to slip into his taps. "Nothing in my contract says I've got to bend over to put my shoes on."

Once, while he was maneuvering into his tap shoes, he shook his head in mock annoyance. "The things you have to do to make four million dollars a year, " he said as the audience chuckled.

It was the first time I heard how much money Sammy earned. I wondered if he was joking. Later, I learned it was true.

Before a dance number, Sammy might joke about having to warn his aging legs.

He'd slap a thigh and say, "Wake up! We're gonna dance now!"

One of his go-to songs was a big band arrangement of *I Can Do That* from the musical *A Chorus Line*. The comic lyrics tell the story of a boy who watches his older sister at her tap class and figures he can do just as well. When she misses a class, he jumps in and takes her place — convinced that if she can learn to dance, so can he. Mr. D sang and danced *I Can Do That* with all the charm and skill he brought to the stage.

His other dance options included a bouncy, full band rendition of *Singin' in the Rain*, and Neil Hefti's *Cute* with the rhythm section and Fip Ricard's muted trumpet.

By the mid-1970s, Mr. D had demonstrated his skills in various instruments, like the vibraphone and piano, less and less during his shows.

***

Sammy returned to Harrah's at Lake Tahoe. During rehearsal, I spotted Gina, the violinist. I hoped for another chance to talk. The opening night shows were cookin'. George featured the band with his own composition called *El Conte*. After Sammy finished his last song, George gave me the downbeat for the lick that kicked off the bows, an up-tempo version of *I Gotta Be Me*. When the curtain came down, George cut us off. I put my music back in order and packed up as fast as I could.

I spotted Gina at the opening night party tables, drinking wine with one of the other string players. She stood out in a crowd—gorgeous face, dark brown eyes, long, silky black hair. I got a plate of food and a half glass of wine and moved near her while trying not to be too obvious. She finished and turned to me with her smile of perfect teeth. "Good show."

"Thank you. You too, Gina."

"You remembered my name."

"No," I said, feigning shame.

Gina chuckled and slapped my arm playfully. "No, you didn't."

"I'm kidding. How could I forget? You are, like, uh, pretty stunningly beautiful."

I glanced around, hoping nobody else heard me. Gina feigned surprise.

"Am I blushing? Thank you, Ricky. Rick."

"I prefer Rick, but everyone calls me Ricky."

I had a plate of crab claw shells. Gina's wine glass was almost empty, her full, luscious lips catching the light as she took a slow final sip.

"Want a refill?" I asked.

She nodded. We got more Pouilly-Fuissé and found a couple of chairs. She lived in Reno but occasionally worked at Lake Tahoe. She got up and said it was time for her to leave. I was just getting warmed up and hated seeing our little "date" end.

***

Billy Preston was with us again at Harrah's Lake Tahoe, one of Mr. D's few guest stars who carried road musicians. Sometimes, we'd eat together or socialize after the shows. I was getting comfortable at "the Rail," the bar outside Harrah's cabaret showroom, cordoned off from the casino by polished brass railing.

I met Sammy's daughter, Tracey, at the rail. I had seen her before visiting her dad backstage, so I introduced myself. B.B. King was performing in the cabaret room. We could see the band well and even hear a little through the windows behind the bar. I figured that since Tracey was the boss's daughter, it might be a courteous gesture for me to offer to buy her a drink. I did, and she accepted. As we started to make small talk, I glanced over Tracey's shoulder as my attention was momentarily diverted. Gary Raynor was arm-in-arm with Peter, Paul, and Mary of the eponymously named group. They were skipping through the casino.

Either he already knows them, or they sure made friends quickly.

Tracey and I chatted about our related interests—mine in police work and hers in the juvenile justice system. She was nineteen, the same as me. We finished our drinks and went our separate ways.

The next night, a half hour before showtime, I checked my drums and music and went to our dressing room. I asked Gary about *Peter, Paul, and Mary.* He told me they were playing the Headliner Room on Mr. D's two off-nights. Gary was a big folk music fan and reminded me of some of their hits like *Blowin' in the Wind* and *Puff (the Magic Dragon).*

Five minutes before showtime, I was waiting on stage left when George came out of his dressing room. We exchanged greetings, and he headed to his podium. I was about to head to the drum riser when Sammy entered, calling me aside with a stern look.

"Ricky, I understand you saw Tracey last night and supplied a little libation."

Oh shit. He's pissed I bought his daughter a drink.

"Yes, Mr. D, I did." Sammy must have noticed the dread on my face. He smiled slowly and then chuckled. "That was nice, babe, thank you." He patted my arm and walked away.

You got me good, Mr. D.

During much of my time with my fellow entourage members—idle time in the hotel, in restaurants, or backstage—somebody was always "startin' some shit," as they put it. When I resisted the razzing, many in the entourage seemed to get a laugh. I guess it was amusing for them to hear the new boy's retort, "Don't start no shit."

The joking and ribbing, no doubt set by the boss's persona, often fell on me as the youngest team member—new to the entertainment business, international travel, and women. Stage manager Jolly Brown, especially, made me his foil, always having a ready answer when I asked a "where" question.

"Jolly, where's my trap case?"

"Atch-your mama's house!"

"Have you seen Fip?"

"Yeah, he's atch-your mama's house!"

I caught on and started giving it back when he left himself open.

"Hey, New Boy, you seen George?"

"Yeah, he's atch-your mama's house."

It was my first experience playing "the dozens," an insult contest popular with blacks. The teasing was often fueled by big Jolly Brown. As I gained confidence, I occasionally threatened to kick his ass. Everyone found that amusing, especially Jolly. If Shirley was around, she'd issue a warning. "You leave him alone, Jolly. Don't mess with Ricky." I sometimes wondered if my father asked Shirley to keep an eye on me, perhaps to ease my mother's worries.

***

After two more nights of exchanging glances during the show, I finally worked up the courage to ask Gina out. To my relief, she said yes. On our off day, she picked me up at the Royal Val, and we went to dinner. The low hum of other diners filled the background as we sat in the dimly lit restaurant. We ordered appetizers and drinks—

Chardonnay for her, a Screwdriver for me—and started trading backgrounds. Gina was from Los Angeles, where she got her music degree at the University of Southern California. She'd moved to Reno two years ago. At one point, she asked me why we wore green ribbons. I explained about the Atlanta child murders, which she'd read about in the newspaper, and told her about Sammy's benefit show with Frank Sinatra. Gina asked me a lot of questions about life on the road. When I told her we were going to Australia, her eyes lit up.

"Australia! How long will you be there?" she asked.

"I think three weeks."

"That's so long. You are so lucky; you must be stoked. And just out of high school."

"Class of 1980. Cleveland Heights High," I said, pausing before asking, "What year did you graduate high school, Gina?"

She smirked. "I'm twenty-six, smart guy."

We laughed, and the conversation returned to Australia.

Gina shrugged. "I don't know why, but I've always loved kangaroos."

"Yeah, kangaroos are cool."

"Bring me one back"

"Sure. I'll book an extra seat and let him sit next to me."

"No, get a female. I want one with a pouch."

After dinner, we walked to Gina's car, and I opened her door.

"Well, that was really sweet," she said.

When I got in, she leaned over and gave me a quick kiss on the lips.

"Just for opening your door?"

She grinned. "Don't push it."

At the closing night party, we said our goodbyes and she gave me her phone number. She said she hoped to hear from me soon. We kissed—this time just a little slower.

CHAPTER
26

After layovers and connecting flights, it took me thirty-three hours to travel from Cleveland to Sydney. Mr. D's engagements had us hopping all over Australia. His extended gigs were at the Hilton Hotels in Sydney on the East Coast and in Melbourne, the coastal capital of Victoria. Sammy's guest star, a gorgeous singer and dancer named Jackie Love, was a local talent. We were both nineteen. Her rather shy persona belied the leggy blonde's dynamic renditions of Don't Rain on My Parade and Sweet Georgia Brown. The crowds loved her. And so did Sammy and his entourage.

During one afternoon in Sydney, several of Sammy's entourage, including me, Fip Ricard, and Jolly Brown, were invited to join the boss on a harbor cruise. Jackie Love came, as did several of Sammy's Australian friends. We boarded a seventy-five-foot luxury yacht near the impressive Sydney Harbour Bridge. It was near the opera house. I recognized the sail-shaped roof shells of the iconic entertainment complex, the same place Sammy recorded *Live at the Opera House*— an album my brother played on.

The yacht had fishing rods and bait available. I had never fished before. Once we were out in the open water, the captain stopped the boat. Fip Ricard gestured for me to join him on the upper deck. He showed me how to bait my hook, then helped me cast off. My line was in the water for about two minutes when I felt several sharp tugs.

"Fip!"

He came over and looked down at my line, then started slapping the railing. "Ahhhh!" There was more laughter coming from below. I leaned over the railing, realizing the joke. Jolly had reached out and was pulling my line. And my leg.

The sun was high, hot, and shimmered off the sea. We were out about an hour when the captain's assistant unveiled a lunch buffet. There were numerous trays of shellfish—crab claws and shrimp on ice—and a full bar. After we ate, some of us doffed our shirts and put on swimming trunks. Mr. D stayed in his cowboy boots, dress pants, and a V-neck sweater, which he wore over a button-down shirt. He spent the cruise chatting with his friends and taking photos.

I spent some of my time chatting with bodyguard Brian Dellow, whose commanding presence hid a mellow but cheeky demeanor. When I told him about my interest in police work, he was dismissive. "Just keep beating those drums, young man, and leave the tough stuff to the grownups. You know the boss is a frustrated cop."

I was surprised to hear that about Sammy. I knew many people were drawn to the allure of police work, if judged only by the number of cops shows on television. Of course, the allure was one thing. Actually delving into that world? It had to take a special breed.

***

After the shows, some of the B-Group members hung out at the Hilton disco, located off the lobby. The drink of choice—Sammy's favorite in Australia was a Pimm's Cup, a British cocktail made with a gin-based liqueur.

One late night after the show, I was with the stage crew—Neil, Jolly, Lester, and Dino. The Pimm's Cup flowed liberally, and many people were dancing. As the music pounded to the dizzying strobe lights, we eyed a trio of apparently local women in their thirties. Judging from their laughter and hoots, they were having a wild girls' night out.

"Those are some live wires," Lester chuckled.

We kept glancing around the room, trading smiles with a few women. One of them kept locking eyes with me—the same one I couldn't stop looking at. She had short brown hair and glasses and looked to be in her thirties with a pretty face. Neil caught on and informed the others. They started prodding me. "Go dance with her. Ask her to dance!"

I did, and soon we were dancing to the Hall and Oates hit, *I Can't Go For That*. Her name was Janet. I bought her a drink. Then I ordered another Pimm's Cup for myself, even though I'd already had too many. I could tell because my sinuses were getting stuffy, and my thoughts were starting to ferment. We danced some more, then sat at a table by ourselves. A few minutes later, some of the lights in the disco dimmed. Janet's friends had drifted out into the hotel lobby, hanging near the exit. They were waving for her to come with them. She got up and started walking toward them but didn't say goodbye.

While Janet talked with her friends, I made my way back to the crew.

"Ricky, what are you doing," Neil asked, faking concern. "She's gotta be forty. And did you see her wedding ring?"

"A little heavy with the makeup," Dino added.

The guys chuckled in unison, but I ignored them. I didn't think she was wearing too much makeup. We stood there watching the girls with curiosity. From their facial expressions and waving arms, it looked like Janet's friends were trying to drag her out, but she wasn't ready for the night to end.

"Looks like she wants to stay," Neil teased, gesturing toward me.

"Ain't that nothin'," Jolly said dismissively,

"Yeah, Miss married-with-too-much-makeup is on a mission," Dino said.

Lester shot me a sly grin. "And Ricky's her objective."

As the disco closed, we moved out to the lobby. The guys peeled off around a corner toward the elevators. I hung back, still watching Janet and her friends. A minute later, her friends turned toward the exit. Janet paused—then turned and started walking back toward me.

***

It's all fun and games between a lonely, married woman and her passing-through-the-country boy toy... until my phone rang.

It was about 2:15 in the morning. I answered with a soft, hesitant "Hello?"

"You've got my wife in there."

Up until that call, Australia had been a blast. Sammy's shows were going well, and the local musicians and crew were fun to work with. But now I was frozen with fear. A surge of adrenaline cleared my sinuses. My heart rate spiked. A few seconds of silence ticked by while I tried to assess the situation—my brain still in a Pimm's Cup fog.

The voice sounded like a guy in his forties. His accent sounded Australian—from their angry region. He spoke again.

"Who do you think you are?"

I tried to keep my face from showing shock and fear to Janet. Clearly, God could not have been happy with me that night, and He had been the last thing on my mind. But it was Him to whom my thoughts quickly turned.

God, what do I do now? How stupid could I have been? Is he in the lobby?

I pressed the phone to my ear so Janet couldn't hear the caller interrogating me.

"Well, young man, what do you have to say for yourself?"

I heard background noise and strained to make it out as I took a deep breath. That voice... I recognized it. It was an English accent. Brian Dellow. Probably part of the prank the stage crew was struggling not to laugh at.

"You guys are idiots," I whispered and hung up.

"Who was that?" Janet asked.

"Just some of the guys joking around."

She smiled. "You must have a lot of fun traveling."

"Yeah," I said, my heart still racing.

Janet and I slept for three hours before I stepped outside the lobby to pay for her taxi, then returned to bed. When I woke up, my thoughts immediately turned to Gina. Later, I found a gift shop selling toy kangaroos and picked out a large one, about two feet tall. It had a collar with a tag where Gina could write its name. The clerk was friendly and offered to package and ship it for me. I also spotted a red tee shirt that I liked for myself—it had "Australia" written on it with a black kangaroo outline, so I bought that too.

Sammy's shorter engagements included a performance at the Twintown Services Club in Coolangatta on the Gold Coast and a telethon appearance in Perth, on the far West Coast, where he donated a horseshoe-shaped diamond ring. While in Australia, some band members bought loose gemstones, claiming the prices were better than at home. I went with them and picked up a ruby and an emerald.

In the meantime, I was also "investing" in long-distance phone calls—a couple to my family, but mostly lengthy conversations with Gina. She said she missed me and wished she could be with me. I told her I missed her too—and I really did. She didn't bring up the kangaroo again, and I didn't tell her that I'd already bought one. Gina shared stories about the shows she was playing, and she asked how Sammy's gigs were going and what I was doing in my downtime. I told her everything I had been doing for fun—the gemstones I'd bought and the cruise. Almost everything.

CHAPTER 27

We were back from Australia, and Sammy kicked off 1982 with a two-week engagement at Harrah's in Reno.

Gina told me she'd pick me up at the airport. My afternoon flight arrived on time. As soon as I exited the jet bridge, I spotted her. Rather, I spotted the toy kangaroo that she was holding in the air while grinning. She rushed toward me, overjoyed. I stood there grinning and shaking my head.

"You actually brought your kangaroo to the airport?"

"Yeah, I thought you'd like that. I was so excited to come and get you that I brought him for the ride."

I pointed at the collar and the tag, which was blank. "I suppose you have a name for him, too?"

"Uh, not yet," she chuckled.

Gina said she was thrilled when the kangaroo arrived. Thanking me repeatedly, she explained she had no idea what was in the big box. With a few nights off before she was scheduled to play Frank Sinatra's show, she invited me back to her place. We grabbed a pizza on the way.

Gina lived in an upscale condominium, and I told her how

much I loved it. She explained that being a full-time house musician had afforded her a good living, but she also taught piano lessons on the side. In her living room stood a beautiful baby grand piano, and next to it, a floor lamp shaped like a treble clef. We ate, and she opened a bottle of wine.

We sat on her sofa in the cozy room, our legs brushing whenever we shifted, and I occasionally ran my hand through her long, silky black hair. At some point, I moved in and kissed Gina. It was slow and easy like we'd been waiting for it. After we kissed, she got up and put on a jazz album on her great little sound system.

"That reminds me, Gina, I got you something. It's in my suitcase out in your car."

I moved toward the door. It was getting late, and Gina suggested I just bring my suitcase in and spend the night. When I brought it inside, she was holding her kangaroo and motioned for me to follow her upstairs. She threw the kangaroo on her bed.

"That's where he sleeps."

Gina showed me where I could set my suitcase. I opened it.

"I hope it didn't break," I said.

I handed her a Grover Washington album called *Winelight*. She hugged me tightly as her body pressed against mine for a beat too long. We went back downstairs, where she played the record softly. We especially liked Bill Withers singing *Just the Two of Us*: "I want to spend some time with you. Just the..."

The air was charged with unspoken attraction. It was getting late, and Gina looked at me.

"Do you want to go upstairs?"

I nodded. In her dimly lit bedroom, Gina moved her kangaroo to the upholstered chair on the other side of the room.

"I don't think he'll mind it over there," she said.

A brief smile flickered between us, but the playful tone from downstairs was gone, replaced by a hush that said more than either of us had. Gina turned back toward me. For a moment, we just stood there, the space between us narrowing. Then she reached for my hand.

***

Morning light spilled through Gina's bedroom window. We moved slowly, not ready to let the moment go.

As I turned to grab my shirt, Gina's eyes caught the scarring on my chest.

I said, "Yeah, I wondered when you'd notice that."

"What happened?"

"I spilled a pot of hot coffee on myself when I was a kid."

"Does it still hurt?" she asked, reaching out and running two fingertips along a discolored area.

"Not anymore. It just looks ugly."

She gave me a sad-faced look—eyes soft, lips just barely pouting. Then she leaned in and tenderly kissed the worst section of scarring. I just smiled, not knowing what to say.

We took showers, got dressed, and headed out for breakfast. Afterward, Gina dropped me at the Ramada Inn, where B-Group was staying. I checked in and had just enough time to catch a cab to Harrah's for rehearsal.

Sammy's special guest was comedian Tom Dreesen. For several years, he'd open periodically for Mr. D. When I first met Tom, we chatted, and he remembered my brother. I told him about my interest in police work, and he surprised me by sharing that he had been a private detective before finding success in the comedy business. Much of Tom's material revolved around him being raised Catholic and his experiences growing up a white kid in Harvey, Illinois, a mostly black neighborhood.

***

A few days into Sammy's Reno engagement, I woke up with a very sore throat. I could tell I had a fever, so I called George. He told me they knew a local doctor and said he or Shirley would call me back. A half-hour later, Shirley called me and said she got me an appointment. I took a taxi to the doctor's office. My temperature was 102 degrees. The doctor said it was a throat infection. He prescribed an antibiotic and gave me enough samples for a complete course, along with several Tylenol pills. Back at the hotel, I felt worse and barely managed to crawl into bed.

Around 3:00 p.m., I was in bed, shivering under the covers. Reluctantly, but wanting to let him know quickly, I called George back to tell him I couldn't make the show. I knew he'd have the house drummer cover for me. I intended to call Gina, but I fell asleep, waking up to the ringing phone around 7:30 p.m. It was Shirley calling to ask how I was doing. I told her I was burning up. She told me to drink a lot of water and said I'd feel better in the morning. She was right. I woke up around 9:00 a.m. and ordered toast and orange juice from room service. Right after eating, I sat on the bed and called Gina.

"Oh my God, Ricky, how do you feel?"

"Better now," I said. "Thanks, Gina. I was going to call you yesterday, but I fell asleep."

"That's okay; I was going to call you, but I didn't want to wake you."

She laughed, and I let out a soft chuckle.

"Did you see a doctor?" she asked.

"Yeah, Shirley got me an appointment really fast. Throat infection. He gave me an antibiotic."

"Boy, you still don't sound too good. Are you sure you feel better?"

"Definitely better than yesterday."

"You should've let me know. I could have brought you something or driven you to the doctor."

"Thanks, but I wouldn't have wanted you to get sick, too."

"Well, that's nice, but if I'm not already sick..."

She let it hang there. I leaned back on my pillow, smiling. And I just knew she was smiling too.

"How did the shows go?"

"Good," she said. "Gerry did a great job on the drums, but I'm sure Sammy and George missed you. I know I did."

"Aw, well, that's sweet. I missed you too, Gina. Okay, I think I'm going to take a shower and try to come back to life. See you before the show?"

"Yeah, and if you need anything, call me."

"Thanks."

***

Word was going around that Sammy would perform at a prison in nearby Carson City on our off day. The inmates at Northern Nevada Correctional Center had sent a letter inviting Sammy to perform—and he accepted.

Holmes Hendricksen provided the Harrah's house orchestra and some stage crew members. We arrived by bus and received visitor badges. Nobody knew what to expect as two prison guards escorted us into the gym. A riser served as a stage for Mr. D while the band was set up on the floor. Additional guards let the prisoners inside.

Tom Dreesen did an abbreviated performance, bringing smiles and laughs to some otherwise hard faces. Sammy came out and spoke of his personal success and accepting the invitation to appear as his way of giving back. The inmates clapped and whistled enthusiastically, as they did after every song. A few of them swayed gently to the rhythm or nodded along. Aside from it being in a prison, the show went as usual, though it only lasted an hour. Afterward, there was no typical chit-chat while packing up. Everyone was eager to get back to the buses. The stage crew members were still loading—lights, microphones, cables. I had all my drums packed and was putting the lid on my trap case. Out of the corner of my eye, I saw an inmate walking straight toward me.

Uh oh.

He introduced himself, said he was a drummer in the prison band and started talking to me about equipment.

He seems nice.

We chatted for a minute. Then he asked me if I wanted to see his drum set. He told me the music room was just outside the gym. "It'll just take a minute," he said. I didn't want to appear dismissive or frightened, so I agreed. He led me out of the gym into an adjacent room with band equipment. Two other inmates were eyeing me, so I gave a quick wave. They nodded, which eased my tension a little. I took less than a minute to look over the drums, an old mismatched kit with bent cymbals and well-worn heads. Still, I nodded in approval. The inmate drummer walked me a few steps back to the gym. Meanwhile, I hadn't heard the guards calling my name. I was only gone two minutes—the crew had already taken my drums away. A peeved guard escorted me outside to our bus. He told me that several months earlier, four convicted murderers escaped. They were all recaptured within weeks. As the bus pulled away, the story made its way down the aisle.

"He went with one of the prisoners to see their band room," I heard someone explain, drawing a few chuckles.

"They were gonna play *Jailhouse Rock*," someone cracked, setting off more laughter.

One of the guys joked that I'd almost been taken hostage.

Maybe not my smartest move.

Five minutes later, when we hit the highway, someone yelled, "Hey Ricky, you want to go back and check out the kitchen?"

***

After Reno, we had a few days off before Sammy's weekend at Heinz Hall in Pittsburgh. It was only a two-hour drive from Cleveland, so I decided to take my Cutlass. George told me Sammy's office would send me a check for the equivalent amount of the airplane ticket to cover my gasoline.

In Pittsburgh, singer and actress Leslie Uggams returned as Sammy's special guest. She earned Emmy and Golden Globe nominations for her role in the 1977 miniseries *Roots*. I had my camera with me backstage when she walked by with jazz singer Joe Williams on her heels. Leslie wore a stunning dress with a plunging neckline.

The whole entourage stayed at the Sheraton at Station Square overlooking the Monongahela River, a ten-minute drive from Heinz Hall. I enjoyed the convenience of having my car instead of relying on taxis. Some of the guys joined me for rides to and from the theater. One afternoon, Lester and I took a ride to see the downtown area, the "Golden Triangle," where three rivers converge. The laughs started quickly. Lester told me that Jolly and Dino wanted to change the name of the stage crew to the technical crew. "Ricky, there ain't nothin' technical about that crew," he joked. Later, I glanced at my gauge and said I had to stop for gas. Lester chuckled when he saw I had a quarter tank.

"Ricky, listen to me. You do not need gas. Brothers in the ghetto drive on 'E' for three days."

CHAPTER 28

I've always liked foreign languages, but I regret not becoming fluent in one. In junior high school, my first choice—Italian—wasn't offered. I picked Spanish instead—a close cousin. I stuck with it for three years, and whenever Sammy's itinerary took us to a Latin country, I looked forward to trying it out. Sometimes I carried a mini Spanish-English dictionary to help me communicate—simple, right?

We were in Mexico City where Sammy was scheduled for five nights at the El Patio Theater. On our first night there, I was out for dinner with the rest of the rhythm section. We had just been seated. When we were together abroad, local culture, cuisine, and history were often topics of discussion. In this case, the subject was bread, specifically the basket of bread rolls at the center of the table. Mickey Laverine pointed out that, unlike in U.S. restaurants, the bread might not be complimentary. Frank Accardo and Gary Raynor weighed in as we waited for our server. We didn't care if it cost extra—we were just curious. I said I would ask the waiter. I knew most of the words, but I didn't remember how to say free in Spanish, and I was eager to show off my skill. I slipped my mini dictionary out of my pocket and into my lap, glanced down, and started flipping through.

F

F—R

F—R—E

There is is—Free: Ocupado

The server, about my age, smiled as he approached. Before he could greet us, I jumped in confidently. I asked him in Spanish if the bread rolls were free. I've been told I have an excellent Spanish accent. When the question rolled off my tongue, a rush of satisfaction washed over me like a warm wave. I had just communicated in a foreign language in a practical everyday setting. My three years of study had paid off. But the waiter did not answer. And his smile dissolved into a look of confusion. I checked my dictionary again. The guys had a good laugh when I explained I'd just asked the waiter if the bread rolls were occupied.

And Mickey was right—we did pay extra.

My next Spanish lesson came during a scary incident I'll never forget. I was riding a hotel elevator in Mexico City with two men and a middle-aged woman. Suddenly, the car jolted to a stop.

Silence.

We looked up and around and at each other. The men rattled off some words in Spanish. I couldn't decipher a single one. One of them pushed the emergency button. We waited a few minutes, but nobody came. The woman was obviously distressed.

I asked, "Hablan ingles?"

None of them spoke English. My face was getting hot, and my forehead was starting to sweat. Panic was setting in, but the woman beat me to it.

She started yelling at the door. "Hay alguien allí? Hay alguien allí?"

At the time, I didn't know what she was saying—but I never

forgot it. The men pulled the doors apart just enough to see that we were between floors.

I said quietly to the woman, "You're okay. Está bien."

What seemed like a half hour was probably ten minutes. Two hotel maintenance men arrived and held the doors open while speaking in Spanish. They offered a hand to help us climb out onto the floor above. I hesitated.

What if the elevator starts moving? I'll be cut in half.

Apparently, the woman had no such concern. Aided by the employees, she quickly stepped up and out. Her relief was obvious. She had been freed from our trap. The rest of us followed. It was a good story for the other musicians. Later, I realized that by calming the woman, I had kept myself from panicking. For years after, I couldn't shake my fear of elevators, especially alone. I took the stairs for the rest of our stay at that hotel. And thanks to the Mexican woman, I never forgot how to ask in Spanish, "Is anyone there?"

While working in Mexico City, I was befriended by a gorgeous hotel employee—about my age, with black hair and a flirtatious smile. Whenever the lobby was quiet, Sofia, who was bilingual, would pause from her work to teach me a few Spanish words or phrases. In the early evening, when she saw me heading off to work, she'd say, "Buena suerte," which means "good luck."

George Rhodes gave me a copy of *La Afición*, a local newspaper that featured a front-page story about Sammy, mentioning his personal musicians. I asked Sofia if she could read it to me in English. She had a break in fifteen minutes and said she would come up to my room. Sofia came up, and we were chatting for a few minutes when my phone rang. It was Sofia's boss. She said she would be coming up to speak with me. When I told Sofia, her smile dropped. She explained she wasn't allowed in guest rooms. I was upset that she might get in trouble. Hurriedly, I propped open my door and grabbed a pen and hotel stationery. I told Sofia to quickly translate some phrases I might need at work.

We may play this song next.

Get ready for the bows.

Good show!

We had about six phrases written when Sofia's boss knocked softly and entered. She explained to me politely but firmly that hotel employees were not permitted in guest rooms. I apologized and told her that Sofia had been very helpful in the lobby. When I mentioned that the phrases were for Sammy Davis Jr.'s show, it caught her attention. I handed her the list. She read it and then looked at me and Sofia suspiciously. I apologized again and said I did not mean to get Sofia in any trouble. The lady seemed satisfied and left with Sofia to return to work. Although we never dated, Sofia came to one of the shows with a girlfriend. Afterward, I saw her in the theater lobby, where she wanted to take a picture with me before she left.

"I enjoyed watching you play the drums for Sammy Davids," Sofia said as her friend snapped a photo of us.

The next day, Sammy's entourage was invited to a bullfight, a major cultural event. Mickey Laverine bowed out, citing the cruelty involved. Most of us, including Mr. D, attended, and he was introduced to a packed arena. He received a huge round of applause. It was my first bullfight, and I was glad to experience the tradition. When it was over, I understood how Mickey felt.

***

I didn't see the incident myself—it happened right at the end of one of Sammy's shows in Mexico. The audience was on their feet, applauding as Mr. D took his final bow. As soon as he went off stage, George cut us off. I gathered my music, put it back in order, and put away my sticks, brushes, and mallets.

Several minutes passed before I noticed some commotion backstage near Sammy's dressing room. Curious, I left the bandstand to check it out. I was surprised to see that Mr. D, now in a casual jacket and cowboy hat, was already set to leave. The show promoter stood beside him, and Brian, Shirley, Murphy, and Dino had circled around them. Mr. D was tearing into the promoter—clearly upset. Apparently, a drunk man in the audience had thrown a small glass at Sammy and hit him on the arm. He wasn't hurt, but his anger was clear. He opened his jacket and revealed a holstered Derringer, a very small pistol.

"I don't carry this for nothing," he told the promoter.

Someone had a rough description of the guy. Dino said he was going after him. Brian tried to talk him out of it.

"We can hold him for the police," Dino said.

"They're not going to do anything," Brian replied.

Dino ignored the warning and jogged off toward the lobby. I followed close behind. We searched but didn't find the guy—probably for the best, considering we were in a foreign country. When we returned, Shirley had everyone laughing.

"If Dino had suddenly stopped, Ricky would've run into him and knocked them both over."

Between Sammy's remaining shows in Mexico, he had an engagement in Phoenix. On our last day at the hotel, I saw Sofia one final time as I was checking out. Her face lit up when she saw me. I walked over to say goodbye. She stepped out from behind the desk, and we shared a quick hug and smile.

She gave me one last "Buena suerte."

"Nice to meet you, Sofia," I said before turning and heading for the door.

After a three-night run in Phoenix, we headed back to Mexico for performances in Guadalajara, followed by sunny Acapulco, where the entire entourage stayed at the same hotel. Most of us were on the same floor. One afternoon, I was on the beach, soaking in the sounds and scenery—the powdery sand, crashing waves, and endless blue sky. Thrill-seekers wearing parachute-like contraptions attached to boats caught my attention. They would get a running start, and then the boat pulled them two hundred feet in the air for a flight over the shoreline. A group of Mexican men in their twenties ran the operation. It was called parasailing and looked like fun. Though I wasn't a fan of heights, I was intrigued. Neil Shurmur, Mr. D's soundman, was going up for a second round. He egged me on. Soon, one of the guides was tightening my harness. In his broken but otherwise impressive English, he explained how to land when my flight was over. By waving colored flags, he would direct me to pull on the line that had the same color ribbon.

It was exhilarating to glide through the air, getting an even better view of the beautiful surroundings and bikini-clad women glistening with Coppertone oil. Meanwhile, Neil's second flight went awry when he landed on some rocks and scraped his leg badly. Despite the mishap, I was hooked and went up a second time. When I was done, I planned to shower and head to the hotel restaurant. They had an open-faced sandwich of baby shrimp in a thousand island-style dressing that I loved. In the hotel, I exited the elevator and ran into Sammy. He had been watching us from his suite, probably with binoculars or through the telephoto lens on one of his cameras.

"Ricky, you ever been that high before?"

"No, Mr. D, I haven't."

"Well, you're smoking the wrong stuff."

We chuckled and moved on.

The next day, on the beach, I sported a tee shirt with a "USA" logo and an American flag background. A Mexican boy, around sixteen, approached me and complimented my shirt. He asked if I wanted to trade, and since his shirt caught my eye and we were about the same size, I agreed. My new tee shirt, which featured the sun radiating into a caricature of a shapely woman—the buttocks emphasized prominently—became a favorite. It was captioned, "Sun Your Buns in Acapulco."

I enjoyed my time on the beach, and I was tanning quickly. White vacationers toasting in the Mexican sun was not lost on Sammy. During some shows, he joked about it. "Sometimes I feel like strutting on the beach past all of the white people trying to get dark and singing, "I stay brown the whole year round!"

CHAPTER 29

It was February 1982. The months flew by, and I hadn't realized it had been over a year since I started working with Sammy. My father reminded me that I was due for a raise. I didn't like the idea of asking for more money, but Dad urged me to ask George about it. My mind was on Sammy's current itinerary, with a quickly approaching one-month European tour.

In the meantime, we returned to Harrah's at Lake Tahoe. Comedian Tom Dreesen was Sammy's guest star.

Backstage, a white toy poodle ran up and down the dressing room hallway. I learned it was a gift from Rip Taylor to Shirley Rhodes, and she'd named it Rippy. I babysat it for a few hours on one of our nights off.

After Lake Tahoe, we left for Europe. Mr. D's first shows were in London. Fip arranged a trip for us to Harrods, where we were fitted for gray slacks and black blazers, which Mr. D paid for. These were to replace tuxedos for some of the European tour dates. The London-based orchestra traveled with us throughout the European tour, including renowned UK musicians like trombonist Bobby Lamb and saxophonist Duncan Lamont. When we wanted to distinguish them from Sammy's personal musicians, we called them C-Group.

After Sammy's show in London, we boarded a plane to Amsterdam. I took my aisle seat. Bernard Wilson, Sammy's valet, maneuvered down the aisle and paused when he reached my row. "Oh, I get to sit next to Miss Ricky." He had the window seat, and I got up to let him through. "You didn't have to move, child," he said with a smile. "I could have climbed over you."

As Bernard sat down, a verbal clash erupted several rows ahead. One of the British musicians had taken Dino Meminger's seat, and Dino insisted he move. The musician didn't understand why he couldn't just pick an open seat. Dino, getting pissed, insisted again, and the man reluctantly complied. We thought that was the end until someone remarked, "Americans always sit in their assigned seats." Another voice added, "It's for identification in case of an emergency."

The first musician interjected, "It's just some American bullshit."

Instantly, Dino was on his feet and looming over the guy. "Hey man, I didn't say nothing about no British bullshit! I'll punch your lights out!"

The musician backed off, and Dino sat down, but the tension lingered in the air.

Bernard leaned in, speaking quietly in my ear. "Miss Ricky, I feel safe now that I know Dino punches lights out."

***

For the European tour, Sammy bolstered his protection team. In addition to his security director, Brian Dellow, he brought along Jack Colen, a friendly police supervisor from the LA Police Department. Brian also added two European bodyguards, including Erik, a muscular and outgoing man in his thirties.

Despite being a beloved international superstar, Sammy

remained wary of the dangers that came with fame, fears rooted in the racist threats he faced during the 1960s. In much of his off-stage time when he was away from his suite, Sammy often carried a concealed handgun. A small suitcase containing two pistols accompanied him on every tour. Lester or Jolly signed the cargo manifest. If legal trouble arose, they would serve as a buffer for Mr. D.

On one leg of the European tour, Sammy forgot a gun in his suite, and the mistake went unnoticed until the hotel manager contacted Murphy Bennett. By then, the entourage had already moved on to the next city. Mr. D sent Brian Dellow in a rented car to retrieve the weapon.

The European tour was fast-paced, with mostly one-night shows. Sammy performed at the RAI Convention Center in Amsterdam, the Casino Kursaal Oostende in Belgium, and venues in Berlin and Hamburg. Many of the theaters were historic gems, some dating back to the late 1800s, while others had been rebuilt after World War II bombings. At each show, Sammy was well-received by his enthusiastic fans.

Midway through the tour, we were invited to a sex show, and most of B-Group attended, as did Sammy. The audience section was small—only about three dozen seats—and the front row was barely ten feet from the stage. I started to head to the back, but a voice interrupted. "Put Ricky in front." I took a seat, front and center, with several people in the group giggling behind me. It was entertainment I never knew existed—graphic intimacy performed by an attractive couple in their thirties. I couldn't wait to leave.

During another leg of the tour, we got an invitation to tour a brothel. There were hallways with small rooms on each side. Girls in their twenties and thirties, generous with their displays of flesh, smiled and beckoned as we passed by. Nobody in the group partook, but later, Mr. D's security man, Erik, hired an escort for the night. He brought her back to the hotel disco. I was sitting with Herbert, an effeminate employee from Sammy's office, who I recently met. As the music pulsated intensely, we watched Erik dance with his rent-a-date.

I turned to Herbert and said loudly, "I like the way she shuffles her feet."

"Yeah! Like a boxer."

Herbert asked about the compensation Sammy's musicians received. "Do you get a per diem?"

I figured Herbert must be a new employee, or he wouldn't be asking.

"No," I answered.

"A well-paid staff is a happy staff."

His questions and comments made me uncomfortable, and I hoped he wouldn't involve me in any suggestions to Mr. D.

We moved on to Copenhagen, where Sammy performed at Tivoli Gardens, one of the oldest amusement parks in the world. I hadn't spoken to my parents since leaving the States, so one afternoon, I called home. My mother asked how I was doing, and I told her about some of the cities we'd visited. We chatted briefly, but when she said something I didn't catch, I realized I'd been distracted—images from the sex show still in my head.

"Be careful," she said and passed the phone to my dad.

After more small talk, he asked, "Have you asked George for a raise yet?"

"Not yet, Dad."

"What are you waiting for?"

"I know, I will, I will."

***

Not long after leaving Copenhagen, I noticed Erik, one of Sammy's European bodyguards, was no longer with us. Later, I found out he'd been arrested at the hotel disco for punching a banking executive during a scuffle.

Sammy performed at the Deutsches Museum in Munich before we moved on to Oslo, Vienna, and Zurich. At one point during this whirlwind of plane travel and performance, I lost my global bearings. After one of the many flights, I woke up as we were landing and dragged myself off the plane. I was in line for customs in Austria and still in a mental fog.

The officer inspected my passport. "Where did you come from?"

It was a simple question.

What country did I just come from?

My adrenaline surged, and my face flushed. My memory was stuck in neutral. The officer stared at me, waiting for an answer, but my mind was blank.

He was getting impatient. "Where did you come from?"

"We've been to numerous countries, sir. I've lost track at the moment."

I smiled, hoping it would ease the situation, but he remained expressionless. I'm sure not knowing where I had just flown in from raised some red flags.

He pointed to one of the stamps in my passport and said gruffly, "You came from Switzerland!"

"Yes, Switzerland. Now I remember. Thank you."

I hope he's not testing me because I still don't remember.

The first three weeks of the tour had been hectic but amazing. In the final week, Mr. D hosted a party for the European musicians. The tour's last performances were in Germany—Munich, Stuttgart, and two nights at Alte Oper (Old Opera) in Frankfurt.

CHAPTER

30

After four weeks in Europe, we returned home. We had three weeks off, and it was a welcome relief from life in the fast lane. I got my usual errands out of the way—dropping off my film at the camera shop and taking my tuxedo, along with the sport jacket and pants Sammy bought us in London, to be dry cleaned. As usual, my mother washed and ironed my tux shirts.

I picked up a couple of local gigs and met up with a few friends. I called Ray and talked to him about asking for a raise, telling him that Dad had been bugging me to bring it up.

"Yeah? What are you waiting for?" Ray said.

"I don't know," I said.

"You're supposed to get a raise since you've been there a year, right?"

"Yes."

"So just go talk to George—he'll be cool about it."

"Yeah, I'm going to."

While still home in Cleveland, I started feeling sick. I ended up with a nasty throat infection, which forced me to skip Sammy's TV appearance on The Tonight Show. It was a big disappointment for both me and my father.

Sammy's next gig was in Las Vegas, this time at the Hilton. Since B-Group was staying there, I called George and told him I wanted to talk. He told me to come to his suite. "George, I've been with the show for over a year now, so I'd like to ask for a raise."

"Oh, you have to ask Sammy that."

I have to ask Sammy personally for a raise?

"Oh. Okay. Thank you, George."

I went back to my room, stewing over the fact that I had to ask the big boss for a raise and trying to think of a reason to put it off again. Instead, I decided to go for it. Sammy's room was on another floor. When I stepped off the elevator, I spotted a uniformed security officer sitting outside a room and knew it was Sammy's suite. I told the guard who I was, and he let me knock on the door. Over the rapid pounding of my heart, I heard voices and laughter from inside before Sammy surprised me by opening the door. He smiled and said, "Ricky. What can I do for you?"

"Hi, Mr. D. Sorry to bother you.

"Yeah, babe, what's up?"

"Uh, George told me I needed to talk to you about a raise. You know, since uh, I've been here over a year now.

"Yeah, yeah, okay," he replied pleasantly. "I'll take care of it, babe."

"Thank you, Mr. D."

Sammy smiled again, turned, went back into his suite, and closed the door. I thanked the security officer and headed back to the elevator, annoyed with myself for waiting so long to do something so simple.

***

It was a treat to occasionally stay at the same resort we were working. It happened again in May 1982 when Sammy returned to Vegas for two weeks at Caesars Palace. Our luxurious suites in their new 24-story Fantasy Tower had sunken jacuzzis and mirrored ceilings in the bedrooms.

Before and in between shows, I might chat with John Sousa, Sammy's plainclothes security officer at Caesars. There was also a uniformed guard who was always backstage.

Gina visited for two days, arriving on Sammy's third night. As soon as the stage crew saw her, the teasing began. Sexual trysts were not uncommon among the entourage—single or married. I eventually learned that Sammy and Altovise, who married in 1971, had an open marriage. Kathy McKee, a former showgirl turned casting agent, knew the details. Years earlier, the bi-racial beauty had replaced Altovise as Sammy's mistress of ceremonies. When Mr. D eliminated the role in 1975, Kathy remained—as his lover. And he had others.

John Sousa would later tell biographer Wil Haygood that Altovise used to call him when heading to Las Vegas to tell Sammy to "get rid of whoever he's got with him."

During idle moments or meals with Sammy's other musicians, it was the latest flings within B-Group that sparked the most amusement, especially those of Dino Meminger. He was single and in great shape. If the topic of oral sex came up and George was nearby, he'd remind us of his aversion:

"You young guys can haul coal with your mouths if you want," he'd joke, laughing heartily.

On Gina's second day, we went for an early dinner at Peppermill, a well-known spot. She looked stunning in blue slacks and a crisp white blouse that complemented her dark complexion. Her glossy red lipstick—bold but classic—drew attention to her full lips and gave her whole appearance a sultry charge I found magnetic and impossible to resist.

Gina attended the second show, and afterward, we went up to my room. I took a quick shower and put on shorts and a tee shirt. We decided to order drinks from room service. Gina wanted a

Chardonnay, and I ordered a Screwdriver. Ten minutes later, we heard a soft knocking. Gina stepped into the bathroom. I opened the door, and the waiter, maybe a few years older than me, smiled, and set down the two glasses.

He started to hand me the check to sign, but then paused. "Are you twenty-one?"

His question caught me off guard. I deflected. "I'm Sammy Davis, Jr.'s drummer."

"Oh, you're with Sammy? Okay," he said, handing me a pen.

I signed the check, tipped him two dollars, and he left. I was flustered for a second—then Gina walked out, and the only thing on my mind was her.

CHAPTER
31

Ray, nine years my senior, was married now with a child, while I was out on the road. We stayed close as brothers, but our lives began to take different shapes. Our time together was mostly limited to when Sammy played Las Vegas, and as always, family, humor, and music were our bond.

Ray needed a week off from his job with the Mickey Finn Show for a minor surgery. Sammy had just wrapped up a gig in Atlantic City and wasn't touring for a couple of weeks, so I was available to fill in. Ray recommended me, and Fred Finn—the show's creator and bandleader—hired me as a sub. Fred was taping a two-night television special at Six Flags Magic Mountain Amusement Park in Valencia, California, a thirty-minute drive north of Los Angeles. I'd seen Ray perform with the Mickey Finn Show before, which reminded me how challenging the music would be to read for the first time.

Each of Fred Finn's musicians portrayed a wacky, costumed character. He provided me with a bright red cap and gown to dress as a high school graduate.

For his television special, Fred had several well-known guests, including Debbie Reynolds and Rip Taylor. Aside from rehearsals and the shows, I didn't interact much with the guest stars. But one night after a show, I ended up in a small group listening to McLean Stevenson—another guest—tell showbiz stories. I recognized him from his role on the television series *MASH*. He told a story about a party at his house, where he caught John Belushi doing drugs in the bathroom. He warned him to stop. Four months later, Belushi was gone—an overdose.

The Mickey Finn Show was a nonstop blend of music and schtick. I got a kick out of percussionist Rudy Rodarte's "Winophone," made from about two dozen hanging wine bottles, each filled with a different amount of water and tuned to specific pitches. Rudy played it with mallets like a xylophone—it sounded as quirky as it looked.

Many of the comic bits centered on Sir Rodney Worthington, a lovable, kilted nitwit played by trumpeter Brian Firth, who really was English. Rodney was adorably shy but always up to something. Fred was the ever-smiling emcee, conductor, and pianist—blond, mustachioed, and dressed in a vest, bow tie, and sleeve garters. He played the straight man, often stepping in to rein in Sir Rodney's antics.

The Mickey Finn Show was as challenging as I'd anticipated. Some of the tempos were blazing fast, with tight segues from tune to tune. Many numbers began with a drum lead-in and launched into ensemble playing that was sometimes zany, but always tight—punctuated by sharp solos and all underscored by Fred's fingers flying up and down the ivories.

***

In July 1982, we had a week off. When my next paycheck arrived, it included a $100 raise, bringing my weekly salary to $700.

Meanwhile, Sammy traveled to Israel at the invitation of Tel Aviv University and the Israeli government following their invasion of southern Lebanon. He told reporters his mission was to visit and console wounded Israeli soldiers with the hope that they would have lasting peace.

When Mr. D returned from Israel, he had an engagement in Atlantic City. Then we were back at Lake Tahoe. Gina picked me up at the Reno airport and took me to the Royal Valhalla, a one-hour drive. I introduced her to Al at the front desk and showed her my room. She was only able to stay for one night because she was playing Wayne Newton's show the next day.

"I wish you could stay longer," I said.

"Me too."

Moments like that reminded me just how hard it was to have anything close to a normal dating life on the road.

***

I was pleasantly surprised to learn that Jackie Love was opening for Sammy at Lake Tahoe. After she impressed him in Australia, he invited her to debut with him in the U.S. I had recently turned twenty, and Jackie and I were about the same age. Off stage, she'd occasionally hang out with us while she was Mr. D's special guest. She was a dynamic, humble entertainer and quick with a smile.

***

In August, we headed off to South America for a mini tour— three engagements in Brazil. Mr. D's first show was in Rio de Janeiro at the Copacabana Palace Hotel, where the entire entourage stayed. The hotel sat just across from the iconic Copacabana beach, its golden sand stretching out to the Atlantic Ocean, which shimmered in blinding blue and white under the afternoon sun.

By the first show of the second night, I was settled in and relaxed. During the second show, Sammy had just finished his third tune, welcomed the enthusiastic crowd, and was monologuing. I looked out at the packed house, but the glare of Sammy's spotlights usually kept me from seeing beyond the first few rows. At that moment, the second row was just fine with me. She was seated just beyond George, right in my view. And she was gorgeous.

What a smile. Wait a second. Did she catch me looking at her?

Sammy turned around unexpectedly, and, having played *Candy Man* countless times, I slipped into autopilot when he called out, "Ching chinga ching chinga." After a few bars of the introduction, I looked at her again. This time, she caught me and smiled. Several times throughout the show, my mysterious fan and I exchanged friendly glances. For Mr. D's final selection, he performed *Mr. Bojangles.*

He thanked his audience and bid them goodnight with his usual farewell of "peace, love, and togetherness."

George kicked off the bows. As the curtain came down, my second-row friend flashed me one last smile and a little wave as if to say, "Goodbye, it was fun."

That was crazy.

A few of the musicians and stage crew were meeting in the hotel lounge for a drink. I had nothing better to do, so I headed in that direction. On my way through the lobby, one of the Brazilian house crew members approached me. I admired how well he spoke English. He told me someone wanted to meet Sammy's drummer and motioned for me to wait. A half minute later, I saw him weaving back through the crowd, trailed by a beautiful woman. When they got close, the crew member left, and she smiled at me. It was the same woman from the second row. She was Brazilian and greeted me in Portuguese.

"Você se lembra de mim?"

I told her I didn't understand.

"Mine name iss Seel-via"

That I understood. I knew that the Spanish and Portuguese languages were similar, so I gave it a try.

"Me llamo Rick."

She chuckled. "Alloh Rrreeck."

This clumsy encounter was taking place in a lobby with lingering audience members waiting for a potential glimpse of Sammy. I looked at Silvia and tipped an imaginary glass to my lips. She nodded. I waved for her to follow me. Off we went to the hotel lounge, where I picked a table for two in a secluded part of the room. Seeing there were no other musicians or stage crew members nearby, I asked Silvia to repeat what she asked me in the lobby. After numerous attempts, I thought I understood. She either asked if I remembered her or recognized her.

"Of course, I remember you," I said. "I never had a beautiful woman, or any woman for that matter, wave to me during the show."

I waited for a smile, but it was too many words too quickly. Silvia got nothing on translation, so I tried my half-ass Spanish. "Sí, sí! Tu estás muy bonita. Muy linda!"

Her face lit up at my compliment. Silvia asked me how many days I was going to be in Rio. I tried my best to explain that Sammy only had one more night. Then, he had performances in São Paulo and Porto Alegre.

Our drinks came, and I signed them to my room. For forty-five minutes, Silvia and I laughed and flirted, struggling to communicate—an attraction growing with each awkward sentence.

We got up and headed for the elevator. As the doors closed, Silvia moved closer, and we kissed. She had a playful, titillating smile as she looked into my eyes. Then—two floors below mine—the elevator stopped. The doors opened, and there she was: the last person I wanted to see at that moment.

"Hi, Shirley."

"Ricky!"

Shirley glanced at Silvia, smiled, and stepped into the elevator.

She turned to the panel and pressed a floor button. Awkward silence followed.

Why aren't the doors closing? The doors are stuck open. Should I introduce her or not?

"Shirley, this is Silvia."

Shirley turned. "Hello, honey."

Silvia nodded and smiled politely. Shirley faced forward again. Finally, the doors closed—mercifully. I glanced over, watching her face for clues. I was pretty sure I caught a faint smirk.

The elevator moved up one floor. The doors opened.

"Goodnight, Shirley," I said as she stepped out.

"Goodnight, baby."

With Shirley gone, Silvia smiled and leaned in close again. Her breath warmed my cheek as the elevator climbed, slow and deliberate. The heat between us rose—no words needed.

***

In September, we were at the newly opened Meyerhoff Theater in Baltimore. Two off-duty cops were working backstage security, including a striking woman in her twenties. I spent some time chatting with the male officer, who looked to be in his forties. He was surprised when I told him I wanted to be a cop.

"You're kidding, right?"

"No, I'm serious."

He shook his head. "You're playing drums for Sammy Davis and traveling the world—and you want to give that up to be a cop? Do you know how many people would trade places with you?"

I shrugged.

He went on. "If you do, you're gonna have a heck of a job transition to deal with. It's not going to be easy."

I'm sure he meant well, but I ignored his comments. The next night, I avoided him and spent my time talking with the female officer, who seemed more accepting of my interest in police work.

**

After Baltimore, Sammy was at Harrah's at Lake Tahoe with Count Basie. Mr. D's plan was for the Basie band to open the show. They would do about thirty minutes, then Sammy would come out and sing two songs. After that, Basie and his rhythm section would exit, and Mickey, Frank, Gary, and I would slip into place. But before the show, George came to me and told me that Sammy wanted me at the drums when he came out. That meant I would play Mr. D's two vocal numbers with Basie and his rhythm section. George didn't say why, and I didn't ask.

Sammy performed cooking arrangements of *My Shining Hour*—the title track from the 1964 album he recorded with the Basie band — and *Ding Dong! The Witch Is Dead*, from the movie *The Wizard of Oz*.

True to form, he tweaked the last line just enough to get a laugh: "Ding dong the witch is dead. Well... it sounded like 'witch.'"

**

Sammy often joked about his soap opera addiction, especially his love-hate relationship with *General Hospital* characters Luke and Laura. He even made a few guest appearances on the show, playing an aging performer. In one episode, he sang *It Had to Be You*. Occasionally, when reminiscing onstage about his time on TV, Sammy slipped into the ballad mid-story, accompanied by just Mickey Laverine on the piano.

A few days into the Harrah's Tahoe gig, I was headed to work in a taxicab. As we crossed Highway 50, I noticed a small crowd gathered on the sidewalk—some kind of emergency. As we crossed the intersection, I turned around to get a better view. Someone had apparently fallen or collapsed, and a few bystanders were kneeling, trying to help. I couldn't see who it was.

When I arrived backstage, something felt off. The usual pre-show buzz was missing. Conversations were hushed. A few minutes later, word spread: Bobby Plater, a Basie saxophonist, had collapsed on his walk to work and had been rushed to the hospital. About twenty minutes later, the news came: he was dead. An apparent heart attack.

Bobby, who was sixty-eight, had been with the Count Basie Orchestra since 1964. The loss hit Basie and his band hard, and we shared the pain. The house band conductor quickly lined up a sub, and everyone did their best to pull it together, pause the shock, and play the show.

For me, it was another career highlight to be on stage with Count Basie and his rhythm section, even if it was just for two songs each night. But what I remember most about that run at Harrah's was passing that emergency on the corner and later finding out it was Bobby Plater having a heart attack.

Fred Finn, the founder and driving force behind The Mickey Finn Show, a long-running music and comedy revue, with drummer Ray Porrello.

Me, subbing for my brother Ray with The Mickey Finn Show, as actress Debbie Reynolds charms a smitten Sir Rodney Worthington (Brian Firth), and trombonist Owen Lienhard looks on.

The lovely actress and singer Leslie Uggams opened for Sammy at Pittsburgh's Heinz Hall in January 1982. She is trailed by jazz singer Joe Williams.

European tour, 1982: Sammy's musicians sightseeing.
L–R: trumpeter Fip Ricard, bassist Gary Raynor, pianist Mickey Laverine, guitarist Frank Accardo.

Sammy signing autographs during the European tour, 1982.

Sammy chats with George Rhodes on a plane during the
European tour.

With Sammy's wife, Altovise, at a party for the London-based band during the European tour.

Sammy chats with friends on a yacht in Sydney, Australia. Road manager Murphy Bennett in foreground.

Sammy leaving his birthday party dinner in Australia, 1982. Murphy Bennett takes care of the bill. Valet Bernard Wilson is seated at right.

Posing with Sammy's bodyguard, Brian Dellow, by the iconic Sydney Opera House.

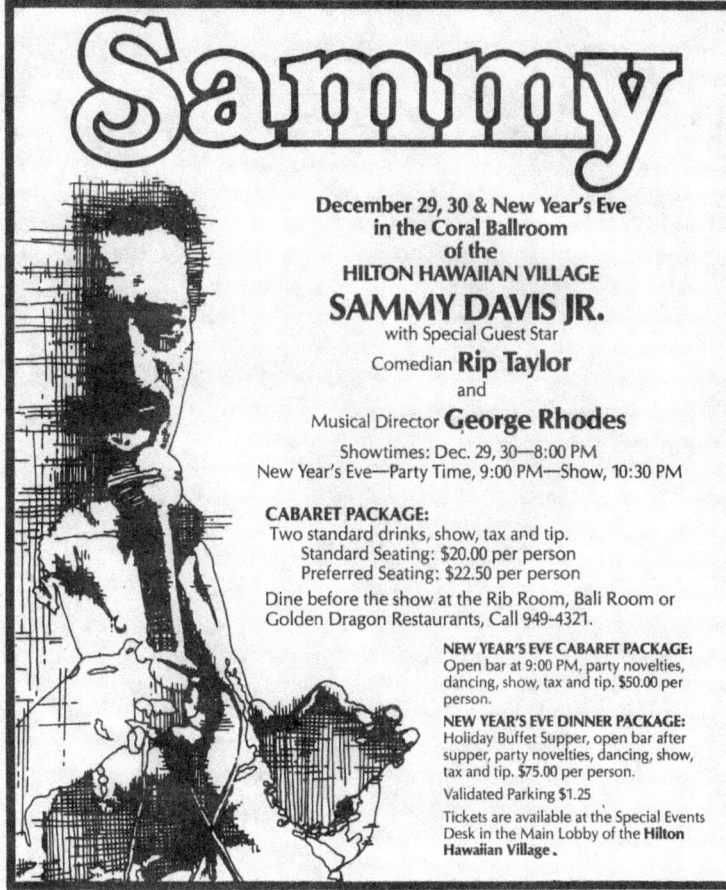

CHAPTER

32

We ended 1982 in paradise—Honolulu. Sammy had a three-day New Year's Eve engagement at Hilton Hawaiian Village. Don Ho, a beloved Hawaiian entertainer best known for his signature song *Tiny Bubbles*, was performing in another showroom at the time.

It was my first time on the island, though we spent almost all of our time at the Village. Late mornings and early afternoons were for the warm sand and the sparkling turquoise waters of the Pacific. After the shows, we relaxed at a Luau-like outdoor restaurant and tiki bar.

Next, Sammy returned to Harrah's Lake Tahoe, where he teamed up with his pal and comedian Bill Cosby, who spun stories about everyday life into hilarity. Their buddy engagement was called *Two Friends* and featured their polar opposite performance and fashion styles. They kicked off the shows in reverse attire: Sammy sporting a collegiate-style sweater and Cos decked out in a tuxedo and sparkling with jewelry. Before the gig ended, each member of the entourage was presented with a "Two Friends" limited edition engagement poster autographed by both stars.

During that engagement, Jolly Brown introduced me to a round, white pill, scored with a line on one side. He said it was a Quaalude or "lude," and it enhanced sex. He didn't mention where he got them from, and I didn't ask. Jolly offered me one for five dollars, and I bought it.

Gina was working in Reno, but she came up to Lake Tahoe to spend two nights with me. I had a night off, so I took her to dinner. We returned to the Royal Valhalla, where I went into the bathroom, took the Quaalude, and washed it down with some wine. Minutes later, I felt myself fading. I sat on the bed, overcome with sleep. Gina asked what was wrong. I told her. She was miffed that I didn't have another Quaalude. But it didn't matter—I fell asleep.

I woke up to my phone ringing. Gina was gone. I turned toward the nightstand, and the clock radio slowly came into focus. It was almost 11:00 a.m.

I slept the whole night and morning!

I picked up the phone. It was Gina.

I felt like an idiot. "I'm sorry, Gina. I'll never do anything like that again."

"Yeah, you were out cold."

I tried to lighten the mood. "You should have stuck around. You could have had your way with me."

Later, I told Jolly what happened.

"Geemonee! You took the whole thing?" He was laughing and shaking his head. "You were supposed to take half, and give her the other half."

"Well damn, Jolly. You never told me that!"

Jolly told some of the other crew members, and they had a good laugh. But everyone knew better than to share it with A-Group. If Shirley had learned what happened, Jolly and I would have gotten an earful. I might have played young and innocent, but he would have caught both barrels.

I can count on one hand the number of times I saw drug use

in Sammy's entourage. I'd seen a few B-Group members snorting lines of cocaine, referring to it as toot, blow, or blow-zo. They joked that I declined membership in that club because I had my sights on someday becoming a cop. And they were right.

The musicians rarely socialized with Mr. D, so I never witnessed any potential drug use on his part. By that time, as I would learn later, Sammy supposedly quit drugs. A few years prior, Frank Sinatra, concerned about the danger of substance abuse, distanced himself from his Rat Pack pal. The rift lasted several years until 1978 when Altovise arranged a reunion. Sammy mended his bond with Frank by promising to quit using drugs.

***

Sammy often featured comedians as guest stars, and Rip Taylor was a favorite. The laughs started as soon as he was introduced. Over the applause, the band launched into a bright rendition of *Happy Days Are Here Again*. As the curious audience watched for the comedian to appear on stage, multiple spotlights crisscrossed the dark room. Rip, with his signature blonde handlebar mustache, entered from the back of the house. Attired in splashy colors and with a bucket in hand, he started toward the stage, tossing handfuls of confetti into the delighted crowd. When he reached his stool and sat, a trombonist blew a gaseous drone. The percussionist kept busy punctuating Rip's antics with sound effects. Even after repeatedly seeing Rip Taylor's act, I still hung out in the wings, laughing quietly rather than joining Sammy's musicians in the dressing room.

Halfway through his act, Rip would break out his box of props and start rummaging. "Holy mackerel!" and out comes a rubber air-conditioned fish. "Oh, big deal," and he displays five giant poker cards fanned out as a flush. He accompanied every punchline with a cackle.

Rip delivered his material rapid-fire, seamlessly moving from his props to one-liners, then cornball jokes and plays on words based on everyday life, like rising costs.

"Everything's going up," he said. "Tattoo is tat-three. And pumpernickel? Pumpernickel's pump-a-damn-dime!" Dino Meminger loved repeating that last line.

One of Rip's jokes had a man pointing to the sky and telling his friend, "Quick, look at the dead bird."

One evening, Jolly and Dino plotted some mischief. Before the show, they attached a rubber chicken to a string. They hid it above center stage and ran the string down to stage left. As soon as Rip said "dead bird," they pulled the string, and the chicken came sailing down onto the stage with a PLOP.

Rip kept a poker face and played along, looking around nervously. "Cover me!" he told the audience. "They're coming toward me." The crowd roared, and so did the crew.

For several months, a few of us in B-Group had been sneaking a high-pitched "What happened?" into casual conversations whenever we could make it fit. A handful of punchlines from our favorite comedians had become running catchphrases among us. "What happened?" was our reference to Rip's story about seeing Cary Grant—the leading man of Hollywood's Golden Age—emerge from a men's room with his trousers soaking wet on one side.

In a squeal, Rip had asked the obvious: "What happened?"

Grant explained he'd been at the urinal, mid-stream, when the man next to him glanced over. Then, in a burst of excitement, the man turned toward him—still peeing.

"Why, you're Cary Grant!"

Rip ended all of his shows by singing a ballad rendition of *Our Love Is Here to Stay.*

I enjoyed Sammy's other opening acts, such as comedians Jimmy Aleck and George Kirby. Willie Tyler and Aaron Williams were ventriloquists who Mr. D featured from time to time. I was amazed at how they could "throw" their voices and make it appear that their mechanical pals were conversing. I learned later that Aaron's other gig was as deputy sheriff for Los Angeles County.

Another entourage favorite, Tom Dreesen, got big laughs with his stories about growing up white in a black neighborhood.

"I played basketball on an all-black team," he'd say. "They nick-named me Spot."

Tom also talked about a tough friend named Goochie who carried a tire iron, the heavy tool you use to loosen lug nuts on a flat tire.

"A lot of the kids bragged that they knew Kung Fu. Well, Goochie knew car-tool."

***

As usual, everyone seemed to have a ball at "The Lake." On our off night, I was with the stage crew at Harrah's. We were hanging out at the Rail. I should have been nowhere near the bar because the following morning was the rehearsal for the relief band. Jolly and Dino challenged me and Lester to a Kamikaze contest. I don't remember who won, but I stopped at four of the vodka cocktails. An hour later, Lester and I poured ourselves into a taxicab and returned to the Royal Valhalla. I lay down, trying to stop the room from spinning around my bed.

After a few hours of sleep, I made it back to Harrah's and sat at my drums for the relief band rehearsal, convinced I was playing just fine. After thirty minutes, George called for a break and motioned me over. With a stern look, he said, "You can't work for Sammy and show up like that." That was it. I'd never make that mistake again.

CHAPTER 33

By the beginning of 1983, my interest in police work tugged at me hard. I did my best to ignore it. The pull of police work was powerful, but my passion for music was deeply rooted.

How do I justify leaving a prestigious job working with a star entertainer to become a cop?

The grind of travel wore me down. I told myself that life on the road wasn't for me, particularly because it made having a steady relationship impossible. I wanted desperately to believe that.

My father bristled at the idea, as did others close to me. Some hinted that leaving Sammy's show would be taking a step *down* on the so-called ladder of success. An uncle tried to dissuade me from becoming a cop.

"Here's how you're gonna die," he said with a grin. He reached into his leather jacket hanging on a chair, clicked open a knife with a large blade, and chuckled. "Some big bastard in a dark alley is gonna stab you."

I smiled and shook my head. He wasn't the type to give good advice, but he had a point.

***

In February 1983, Sammy joined Frank Sinatra and Dean Martin for a charity performance. Dubbed "Valentine's Love-In II," the show was a reprise of Frank's 1980 fundraiser for the Palm Desert Hospital in his hometown of Palm Springs, California. His daughter Nancy was also on the bill. The event was held in the Canyon Hotel's convention center room.

Before rehearsal, I milled around in a corner of the room with Lester Mornay and Frank Accardo. I had my little 35mm point-and-shoot camera with me. Stage crews wrapped up their work while hotel staff decked out the room in pink glittery fabric, heart-shaped foil balloons, and pink carnations on every table. Sammy and Dean were already there. I sat next to Frank Accardo. We were talking about Italian food, and he told me about a pasta recipe in which a cup of ricotta cheese is stirred in. Our attention shifted to Sinatra walking in with a group of several men. There was a quick-moving guy in his thirties, maybe five feet seven inches tall, pointing and directing others. We wondered who he was. Frank turned to me. "A bodyguard?"

"He looks kind of small to be a bodyguard," I said.

"Maybe he knows car-tool," Frank joked.

Witnessing this Rat Pack reunion was another career highlight and I wanted to preserve the moment. As the legendary pals stood chatting and joking, I approached quietly, my camera ready for a candid shot.

I overheard Sinatra say quietly, "He's gonna take a picture with that little thing?"

I snapped two quick photos, smiled, and sat back down.

The Valentine's Love-In event was a $1,000-a-plate event featuring a five-course Italian dinner and champagne. The guests included former President Gerald Ford and movie stars Jimmy Stewart, Kirk Douglas, Gregory Peck, Robert Wagner and his wife Jill St. John. The knockout blonde actress Angie Dickinson was there as well. I knew her best from the television series *Police Woman*.

During the gig, I met Frank Sinatra's longtime drummer, Irv Cottler, and his bassist, Gene Cherico. Cottler was known for his unobtrusive, rock-solid, and tasty style. The band was from Los Angeles and included trumpeter Conte Candoli. I usually had a separate drum riser. This time, I shared one with the trumpet section. Conte kept time with a heavy foot, and I struggled to ignore the reverberations. Sammy performed two songs by himself. Afterward, I watched Dean Martin's routine, which included jabs at Sammy being black. The teasing between Rat Pack members made the audience howl.

Dean joked about Sinatra's Mafia connections. "Frank always remembers me on Valentine's Day. Last year, he sent me a heart. And it was still beating!"

***

After the Palm Springs benefit, Sammy headed to Detroit for performances at the Fisher Theater, with Billy Preston opening the show. One evening, my cousin, who lived nearby, came with her parents. I brought her backstage, and at my request, Sammy posed for a picture with us.

Mr. D's bodyguard for the trip was a former Secret Service agent. I often chatted with him outside Sammy's dressing room between shows, where he shared stories from his time on the presidential security detail. Alongside him, two plainclothes Detroit police officers provided security.

From Detroit, Sammy moved on to the Stanley Theater in Pittsburgh, then the Shubert Theater in Philadelphia. Crooner Billy Eckstine joined the bill—a friend of Mr. D dating back to Sammy's earliest days with the Will Mastin Trio. Everyone close to Billy simply called him "B." Like Sammy and George, Billy shared a close, decades-long bond with his conductor, Bobby Tucker. After his first few tunes, Billy would pause to introduce "Tuck" and joke that their friendship had lasted longer than any of their marriages.

Onstage, Billy was a smooth baritone in his sixties and in fine form. Offstage, however, he was loud, a bit crass, and loved to needle others—especially Shirley Rhodes, whom he affectionately called "Butterball." Her quick flashes of mock anger never seemed to slow him down.

On one of our off nights, Sammy took the entourage to dinner at an Italian restaurant called Mama Yolanda's in South Philly. Billy Eckstine was there, as was Mr. D's pal, Jerry Blavat, a well-known disc jockey. The restaurant owner, an Italian woman in her seventies, who everyone called Mama, greeted us. She showed us to a private room with a big table.

After we got settled, Billy announced, "I've got to piss."

None of us knew where the restrooms were.

The room broke out in laughter when Billy turned to me and said, "Ricky, go ask Mama where she squats."

"You stay right there, Ricky," Shirley instructed, then turned to Billy. "B, you can hold it till the waiter comes."

"Whatever you say, Butterball."

CHAPTER
34

My left wrist had been hurting for several weeks. My sister, an assistant to a doctor at the renowned Cleveland Clinic, made me an appointment with their sports medicine department. Meanwhile, I could feel a fascinating life chapter winding down. I wanted to turn the page, but it seemed unnatural and illogical—a bizarre career transition. But something about my plan—however strange—kept pulling at me. Deep down, it felt right, even if I couldn't explain why.

A few close friends and family thought I was throwing away my talent. My dad's silence hit the hardest. For him, the musical success of his sons was a dream come true, and my plan to leave the stage derailed that dream. He didn't try to talk me out of it, but he didn't encourage me either. My mother supported me. In her conservative and risk-averse world, life as a musician was unstable.

"You have to have something to fall back on."

Still, the misgiving about putting in my notice to leave the employ of the greatest entertainer in the world—to become a cop— tortured me for several months.

How do I rationalize it? Will I regret my decision?

I wrestled with it for months. Leaving Sammy's show—the biggest break of my life—to become a cop? It sounded insane. But still... I couldn't shake the feeling it was what I had to do.

***

The man was a giant in the drumming world and my father's longtime friend. He'd mentored my brother and helped Ray land the drum chair with Sammy. Louie Bellson meant a lot to me. I wrote to him to share my plans. I wanted him to hear it from me, not out of duty, but more about easing a quiet guilt I'd been carrying—something like what I felt with my father.

Louie's reply was concise and helpful: "We must be happy in life."

Two friends from home—one a cop, the other a drummer—told me something similar. "You're young. Give it a try. If you don't like police work, you can always go back to music."

Their advice gave me the mental traction I needed. A few weeks later, in April, I met with George Rhodes and told him I was leaving the show. He wasn't surprised. Though I loved playing drums for Sammy Davis, Jr., I never hid my interest in police work. Everyone knew I was the kid who wanted to be a cop. George needed time to find a replacement, I reasoned. I told him I'd stay through June. He appreciated the gesture.

Sammy was in the process of scheduling performances in Italy in August. He saw me outside his dressing room.

"Hey babe, why don't you stick around a bit and come with us? See the old country."

Italy. With Sammy Davis, Jr.

Part of me wanted to say yes. But I'd already scheduled wrist surgery, which I explained to Mr. D. Neither Sammy, George, nor any entourage member showed any negativity or ill will toward my decision. But now, I was just a pending vacancy to fill. It all seemed so matter-of-fact—so routine. Road musicians came and went. They stayed for five or ten years, maybe less, maybe more. They left for various reasons, often the instability of life on the road. For me, it was time.

**

In May 1983, Sammy was back at Harrah's in Reno for a one-week run. Gina worked the shows, and I couldn't help but sneak glances at her as she played and enjoyed Mr. D's performance. We spent a lot of our off time together eating meals and walking in the casino district downtown, and in the city's many parks. I told her I'd handed in my notice. She wasn't surprised, given our past talks about my interest in police work. With Gina's every smile, I felt a pang of guilt, knowing I'd soon be back in Vegas with Sherry.

**

A week or so later, Sammy played the Aladdin in Vegas, and B-Group was back at the Ambassador Inn. I was sitting in the coffee shop, eating and joking with Frank, Dino, and Lester. Sherry was on a break and came in and sat with us. During that gig, I found myself spending more time with her. We had an obvious attraction, not the least of which stemmed from our age difference of fourteen years. Recently divorced, I sensed that I was more of a pleasant distraction for her. Unlike with Gina, I was confident Sherry understood our relationship was temporary—built on friendship and pleasure.

She suggested we take a ride to see Lake Mead. We planned to leave at 11 a.m., drive to the lake, and stop for lunch on the way back. But I didn't wake up until 10:45. I slowly opened the curtains, but the blinding Vegas sun made me squint, so I left them closed. I didn't want to miss Sherry in the shower, so I splashed water on my face and brushed my teeth. She knocked, and I opened the door to her flashy blues, a quick kiss, and an inquisitive look.

"What time did you go to bed?"

Before I could answer, she peered around my room with mock suspicion and a chuckle. "Are you at least alone in here?"

"I had a few drinks with Mickey, Frank, and Gary," I said. Sherry flung my drapes open, and I turned away from the burst of sunlight. "I set my clock radio for 10:00, but for p.m. instead of a.m. I have to take a quick shower to wake up."

"Oh, getting naked and going in the shower, huh? You're a young tease."

We laughed. I grabbed my clothes for the day, turned on the light and exhaust fan on in the bathroom, and closed the door. Sherry said something loud about our plans for later. I didn't catch it all and opened the door for her to repeat it.

She said, "Maybe I can maul you when we get back if we have time."

We laughed again.

"Now, who's being a tease? Want to take a shower with me?"

"No. And hurry up, drummer boy, we have to get going."

Sherry flipped on the TV and sat on the bed. I closed the bathroom door and started the shower. The water got hot fast. Just as I stepped in, I heard my phone ring. I had a pretty good idea it was Gina.

"Don't get it!" I yelled.

"Okay!" Sherry said.

Two minutes later, I toweled off and opened the bathroom door a crack.

"Ready in a few," I said.

"Call Gina," Sherry yelled.

I stepped out. "What?"

Sherry didn't look at me. "Call Gina. That's who called."

She turned, and we faced each other.

"But Sherry, I said, 'Don't answer it.'"

"No, you said, 'Get it.'"

There was a pause, longer than it needed to be.

"It's okay," I said. "Maybe you didn't hear me over the shower."

She gave me a look that said, I heard you just fine.

There was no point in arguing. I'd deal with Gina's questions later. And I knew she'd have a lot of them.

On the ride out to Lake Mead, I thought Sherry might ask who Gina was, but she didn't. Maybe she already knew. She probably figured I had someone else, maybe more than one. I was twenty, on the road with a star entertainer, and she'd likely heard me and the guys joking around at the Ambassador. She'd lived enough to see that kind of thing before. And maybe, in her own way, she'd decided not to ask questions she didn't really want answered. Instead, we talked about me putting in my notice to leave Sammy's show. She knew it had been a tough decision and was sympathetic.

"Look," she said. "If it's something you really want to do, you have to do it. I mean, it's dangerous, but it's a solid job. And we need good cops."

We traded a quick smile.

"If it makes you happy," she said, "then I'm happy."

I would've hugged her if she hadn't been driving.

The next day, I called Gina. She didn't answer. I left a message asking her to call me and gave her the number for the Ambassador Inn, even though I knew she already had it. I didn't know what I'd say when she called back. But I knew it was coming—and I knew she'd be hurt. Or pissed. Or both. And I couldn't blame her.

With Count Basie, backstage at Caesars Palace in Las Vegas.

Lester Mornay and Murphy Bennett enjoying a Lake Tahoe
party hosted by friends of Sammy's stage crew.

Comedian Tom Dreesen, a favorite of Sammy and the entourage, signed a photo to me: "May you grow to be as great a drummer as your brother (and better looking)."

George Rhodes reviewing music during a rehearsal.

Showing Sammy's bodyguard, Brian Dellow, a thing or two.

With gorgeous Australian singer Jackie Love, Sammy's
special guest. Lake Tahoe, NV, 1983.

Sammy at rehearsal for Frank Sinatra's Valentine's
Love-In II fundraiser in Palm Springs, CA, 1983.

CHAPTER
35

A week after Sammy's Vegas run at the Aladdin, he was booked on The Tonight Show—a dream gig for me. I was nervous but looked forward to being on that legendary show with star musicians I revered, like trumpeter Conte Candoli and tenor saxophonist Pete Christlieb, both of whom often worked with Louie Bellson.

Gary and I arrived at LAX on the same flight and rented a car. Gary drove. We happened to stop at a red light next to an LAPD patrol car. I noticed their motto—*To Protect and Serve*—and wondered what kind of call they might get next.

That evening, dinner was at *Fatburger*. Jolly recommended the famous burger a week earlier. "Hey, Paleface," Jolly had said. "You gotta try a Fatburger when you're in LA."

The following day, we were off, and I spent a few hours tagging along with Lester, who was running errands for Sammy and picked me up in his black Cadillac station wagon. It looked just like a hearse, with a license plate that read, "MR D."

Lester and I reminisced about some of B-Group's old mischief. We laughed about two incidents from Sammy's European tour. One time, Brian Dellow and Neil Shurmer tied me up while I was wearing a new tracksuit. They shoved me into my own shower, turned on the water, and told me my brother was on the phone, long distance, of course. He wasn't. In another episode, Jolly and Dino engineered a "burglary" of Lester's hotel room. Dino entered Lester's unlocked patio door from an adjacent room and took a couple of his dress shirts. Les and I planned our revenge. Around 3:00 a.m., after making sure Dino and Jolly were asleep, Les and I stalked the hallway around B-Group's rooms, then pounded on their doors and made our escape.

"Knockers forever, Rick," Lester said with a grin as he steered the hearse.

We headed into a rough-looking neighborhood. I glanced out the window and saw a big dog roaming loose while pedestrians eyed us curiously.

As Lester pulled into the little parking lot of a nondescript two-story building, he said, "Ricky, the next time you see Shirley, do not ask her about Rippy."

Rippy was the toy poodle Rip Taylor gave her. Before I could ask him why, Lester parked the car with a quick turn of the wheel. There was a man in his forties standing on the corner, staring at us. Lester started to get out. I opened my door to follow, but he said, "Stay with the car. I'll be right back."

The man on the corner shouted, "Hey! What's the D stand for?"

Lester didn't miss a beat. "Deadly!" he barked, then disappeared inside.

I shook my head, smiling, and sat there hoping he hadn't pissed the guy off. Lester returned in two minutes, and we had a good laugh. He didn't tell me what he had to do in the building, and I didn't ask. I did ask about Rippy. Lester told me the little dog had been in the Rhodes' backyard when a coyote jumped the fence and killed it. Coyotes came down from the hills and went after small pets. I felt awful for Shirley.

While we were in Los Angeles, George invited Fip, Gary, and me to his home for pizza. He had a big music room with a high ceiling and a grand piano, where he worked on Sammy's arrangements. The walls were covered with framed photos of musicians and celebrities.

"You have a beautiful home, George," I said.

"I wish I could enjoy it more."

I thought about Gina for a moment.

I guess that's life on the road.

The next day, we arrived at the NBC studios in Burbank for rehearsal.

I'm here in the studio! It's the Tonight Show!

Ray had often appeared with Sammy on the show, but this was my first time.

Ed Shaughnessy's double bass drum setup was a little bigger than mine—two extra tom-toms and cymbals set a bit higher. I didn't adjust anything for the two songs we played. The rehearsal flew by.

During the show, Ed sat to my left, perched on the corner of the drum riser. He didn't watch me play, which was a relief because I was already feeling the pressure of playing that legendary set. While Mr. D was singing, he moved right in front of the band. When the camera swung toward us, I pictured my parents at home, glued to the TV and smiling.

Johnny Carson's other guest was actor James Sikking, who played Lt. Howard Hunter on *Hill Street Blues*—one of my favorite cop shows. I couldn't wait to tell Dad all about it the next day.

A week later, I finally reached Gina. She was upset.

"Gina, I'm sorry. She was just a friend in Las Vegas," I said.

It was partly true. I didn't feel the same way about Sherry as I did about Gina. But it was also a lie. Sherry wasn't just a friend.

"If she was just a friend," Gina said, "then why did you apologize? And how many friends do you have?"

Her voice cracked—angry, hurt, or both.

I didn't have a good answer. I just said, "I'm sorry."

She hung up.

I sat there in silence, wiping tears from my eyes.

CHAPTER
36

We were back in Las Vegas. Ray had recently been hired as the drummer for Caesars Palace. I started hearing chatter about negative changes in the music scene. The concern stemmed from shows replacing live bands with recorded music and synthesizers.

"The handwriting is on the wall," one musician lamented.

By the early 1960s, culture and technology were reshaping American entertainment. The number of American homes with television sets was increasing. The aging swing-era population led to the curtain slowly falling on the big bands. Rock and roll groups like the Beatles and the Rolling Stones became popular with teenagers who would define the music industry for a coming generation.

In her book *Played Out on the Strip*, author Janis L. McKay wrote that changes began in Las Vegas in 1966 when industrialist Howard Hughes settled there. He purchased numerous resorts, which slowly reduced the control and influence of mobsters. Other independent developers, including Jay Sarno and Steve Wynn, changed the scene as well. Around the same time, a rewrite of Nevada's gaming law allowed corporations to buy casinos. The executives recognized the potential for profit and growth and started moving in. The pattern continued with the mob's bankrolls unable to compete with corporate capital.

Before the corporations took over, the biggest showrooms had a "star policy." Their rosters of A-list entertainers were guaranteed a minimum number of weeks to perform, and their compensation included the use of the house orchestra. It was back when resort owners treated major entertainers with great respect and valued them for their ability to bring in crowds.

When the shows ended, the audience spilled into the casino, where the resorts earned most of their money. I remember hearing that slot machine profits alone covered a resort's operating expenses. The tourists gambled, inevitably trying, almost always in vain, to out-bet or out-luck the house.

But more changes were coming to Nevada resorts. Around 1983, corporate bosses began cutting costs by no longer providing full orchestras for top headliners. Consequently, over the next several years, many stars cut down on their number of live musicians. Diana Ross reduced her band to a rhythm section, a synthesizer, and four violins. Others were coming in entirely self-contained.

As the years passed, house musicians were laid off with increasing frequency. Some looked to L.A. for studio gigs. Others taught music, took side jobs, or switched careers entirely. A few became Realtors. As the trend continued, one veteran musician motioned to his two dozen peers during a 1984 house band rehearsal and said, "You're looking at a dinosaur."

***

I was home, and it was my second-to-last gig. It was also said to be Sammy's first time performing with a major symphony orchestra. The show took place at northeast Ohio's venerable Blossom Music Center, with the famed Cleveland Orchestra. Mr. D's performance was the season opener for their Summer Pops Concerts. Blossom's amphitheater seated six thousand under its pavilion, and the adjacent lawn could hold twice as many on blankets and lawn chairs.

During rehearsal, I met guitarist Tommy Morell, who had worked with Sammy for years while my brother was on the show. He was filling in for Frank Accardo, who was getting married that weekend.

Later, Sammy tap danced to a dramatic arrangement of the Prologue to *Pagliacci*. But most of the show stuck to his usual arrangements, along with some recent additions like the Toreador song from the musical *Carmen Jones*, an African American adaptation of the opera *Carmen*. Sammy acted in the play in the 1950s.

My family came to the show. Maybe because of that, Mr. D performed his voice-and-drum routine. During the ten-minute medley, it felt a little awkward accompanying Sammy while a hundred internationally renowned musicians sat silent.

My father invited the entire entourage to our house for dinner. Sammy came and noticed the photo I had taken of him years earlier at the Front Row Theater.

He referenced his longer hair. "Look at that doo," he chuckled.

For me, and no doubt for my father, it was a bittersweet and ironic evening. It was the first time we had Sammy at the house, but I was leaving his show in a month.

***

It was June 1983, and Sammy was doing two weeks at Harrah's Lake Tahoe. Comedian Billy Crystal was his guest opener. As usual, B-Group was staying at the Royal Valhalla overlooking the blue and serene lake. When I checked in, Al told me a young woman dropped off an "interesting item" for me. I had no idea what it might be. He turned and reached into a back room. When he turned back, he was holding Gina's kangaroo. Al must have noticed the look of heartbreak on my face.

"I won't ask," he said.

He handed me my key and the kangaroo, and I headed to my room. I passed Dino in the hallway.

He chuckled. "Hey, P-Baby! Is that your date for tonight?"

I ignored him and fumbled with my key to enter my room. As I set the kangaroo on the table in the kitchenette, I noticed that Gina had written a name on the collar tag: JERK.

The following day at rehearsal, I sheepishly scanned the string players. Gina wasn't working the show. It was a relief.

Opening night came and went. The next day, I got up late and called her—half-hoping she wouldn't answer. I was still figuring out what to say when she picked up.

"Hello," I said.

"Hi." A pause.

We made some small talk. Gina was playing with Tony Bennett and Rosemary Clooney at the time.

I changed the subject. "I'm glad you finally named your kangaroo."

She chuckled softly, and I was relieved. We agreed to meet for lunch in a few days.

During the first week, the Harrah's stage crew organized a softball game with some of Sammy's entourage and Billy Crystal. My friend Dick Conway, Sammy's house security man, and I played too. They had me pitch, but when I gave up too many runs, Billy replaced me as pitcher. For a couple of hours, the fun kept my mind off the fact that this was the last gig of my two and a half years working for Sammy. Meanwhile, George had found a replacement.

Late Tuesday morning during the second week, I called for a cab to meet Gina for lunch. She was driving up from Reno. I brought the kangaroo with me, hoping she would take it back. I arrived early and sat the kangaroo in the chair beside me. Gina walked in, spotted it, and smiled. Again, I felt a sense of relief. Neither of us was very hungry, so we ordered a couple of appetizers. We talked quietly, sharing what had been left unsaid.

"I was wrong," I said.

"I'm not naive, Rick. I knew what life on the road probably meant. But that call—having her answer—it stung."

I didn't know what to say, so I tried to lighten the mood. I asked her to take the kangaroo back.

"I'm not a stuffed animal-on-the-bed kind of guy," I joked. "He'll wind up in a closet."

She grabbed the kangaroo and hugged it. "No, no, he can't live in a closet," she laughed with mock concern.

I paid the bill and offered Gina five dollars for gas money for coming up from Reno. She wouldn't take it. There was a payphone inside the restaurant lobby. I was going to call for a taxi. Gina offered to drive me back to the Royal Val. When we arrived, she got out with me, and we both felt the weight of goodbye hanging between us.

I motioned toward the kangaroo in the back seat. "Maybe you can, uh, you know, give him a new name."

We chuckled. She got back in her car to leave and started crying a little. I played it tough—until I got back in my room.

***

While chatting with George Rhodes, I learned that Sammy's proposed shows in Italy had been canceled. Later in the week, George introduced me to my replacement, Clayton Cameron. Seeing him was a reminder that the decision I'd agonized over was finally real. Sammy's closing night arrived, and it was mine as well. I tried to hide my sadness, which had built up over several months of uncertainty about whether to leave.

Sammy was about two-thirds through the second show of closing night when he paused. "This is a mixed-emotion night for us."

It caught my attention. When he continued, I knew he was referring to me.

"We are saying goodbye to a member of our musical family. He has been with us for two and a half years, and he's decided to pursue another career. May God put His arms around him. Ladies and gentlemen, I speak of my drummer—Ricky Porrello."

The audience applauded, and I stood, feeling a lump in my throat. Over the clapping, I heard, "Rickeee! Rickeee!" from some of the musicians and crew. I forced a smile, nodded toward Sammy and the audience, then sat down.

The applause quickly trailed off, and Mr. D continued. He turned back to the audience and shook his head in mock envy.

"Twenty years old," he said, and there was scattered laughter. "Ricky can have seven careers. I'm stuck! It's *The Candy Man* until I die."

There was more laughter, and then Sammy called for *I've Gotta Be Me*. The lyrics speak to one's drive to pursue their dreams and goals despite challenges. George gave the downbeat, and Sammy started singing:

"Whether I'm right, or whether I'm wrong..."

The following morning, I climbed into the shuttle for the ride to the airport. My drums were being shipped home separately. For the next hour, I gazed out the van window, much in a trance, as we left the breathtaking region of Lake Tahoe and descended from the tranquil, snow-capped Sierra Nevada mountains into downtown Reno.

In seven hours, I would be back in Cleveland.

CHAPTER 37

After two and a half years on the road, I was back at my parents' house, sleeping in the narrow and lonely bed of my childhood. My father rarely voiced his feelings, but I could tell what he was thinking—and it made me wonder.

Was this a riches-to-rags story? Had I made a mistake?

Some family members and friends thought so. They saw the excitement of international travel and the prestige of working with a superstar. What they didn't see—couldn't see—was how strongly I felt pulled toward something else. I was shackled by an intense desire—a calling, really—to become a police officer. Very few people close to me offered encouragement. I had to be my own cheerleader.

While recovering from wrist surgery, I began researching college law enforcement programs. If I was all in on a police career, I wanted the advantage of education. I got reacquainted with friends and fellow musicians and was soon back to playing drums at parties.

But after those gigs, I had trouble falling asleep. Closing my eyes brought swirling memories and concerns about the past and lingering uncertainty about the future. Then there's a knock at my parents' front door. I open it, and there she is—the girl from Rio—

holding the hand of a two-year-old boy. He has dark, curly hair. I stare at him. There's something familiar in his eyes as he looks back at me with sadness. Then I wake up—with great relief. It was just a dream. One of many.

In another, George Rhodes calls me—just like I secretly wished he might do in the future—and asks me to fill in on drums for one of Sammy's weekend engagements. But when I show up, things fall apart. Cymbal stands collapse. My sticks pass silently through the drum heads. Nothing works. Maybe it was a message—my subconscious reminding me to keep moving forward. Don't reach back for the life you chose to leave.

In the months following my return home, many relatives, friends, and acquaintances asked me about my time on the road with Sammy Davis, Jr.

"What was Sammy like?"

"He was an incredible entertainer, and his shows were fun to play. Every show was a little different. But other than on stage, the musicians spent little time with him. When we did see Mr. D, he was often a teaser, a ball-buster."

"Did you have a girl in every port?"

I just laughed.

Inevitably someone would ask, "Did you meet Frank Sinatra?"

"Well... sort of. No, not really. Actually, yes—I did meet Frank Sinatra."

Someone said, "You should write a book." A few months later, another person repeated the suggestion.

Yes, maybe I should write a book.

Over the next year, in my spare time, I wrote down as many memories as I could recall. I took detailed notes, prepared outlines and chapter summaries, and gathered my favorite photographs. I even came up with a working title—*On the Road with Sammy*. But the book wasn't meant to be. At least not yet.

Then came my twenty-first birthday—the minimum age to become a police officer in Ohio. I pored over a map of Greater Cleveland, using a marker to outline dozens of cities, townships, and villages—each with its own police force. I wanted to work in an east-side suburb near Cleveland Heights, where I grew up. I figured if I avoided busy places like the City of Cleveland, I could still play drums on the side. Music was still my passion, and I wasn't ready to give it up.

Unlike music, police work was a world I knew nothing about. I had no family history to lean on. Neither my father nor my brother could guide me or help me. I didn't have years of training or experience. Starting fresh, with no mentor and little support, was daunting. Even my mother's cousin, a Cleveland Heights police officer, didn't take my interest seriously.

As I filled out forms for a community college criminal justice program, a memory came to me: my seventh-grade teacher, a nun, visiting me in the hospital after I was burned. I wondered if talking to her might help me sort through my doubts. One afternoon after school, I met her in her classroom. We talked about how uncertain I felt about switching careers, and she shared stories from her own life. I was surprised to learn she enjoyed water skiing.

"Do you think we sit around praying all day?" she joked.

Then she suggested I start reading the Bible—something I hadn't really done despite my Catholic upbringing. She stood, walked over to a shelf, and grabbed a full-size Bible.

"Here," she said, handing it to me as a gift. It was my own copy—lifted straight from the school.

I read it off and on, usually when I felt lost or in need of direction. At times, it gathered dust on my nightstand—but I always returned to it. It gave me comfort, wisdom, and practical guidance when I needed it most.

***

The first police entrance exam I took was on a Saturday morning in a small town's high school cafeteria. When I pulled into the parking lot, it was packed. At first, I thought it was a school event, but inside, the room was filled with applicants. I got in line to check in. There were a dozen young men ahead of me and one young woman. A few more joined behind me. The test covered general knowledge—basic science, math, history—and simple law enforcement scenarios. I finished, handed in my paper, and walked back outside with several others. We were all quiet, probably just as nervous as I was.

One hundred and fifty people were competing for two jobs! Becoming a cop was going to be tougher than I'd thought.

Ten days later, the test results arrived in the mail. I scored 76% and ranked 109th on the eligibility list. Disappointed but not defeated, I took another exam two months later. The results were similar. Most departments gave extra points for college degrees, military service, or police academy training—none of which I had. I realized I needed to widen my search beyond the east side. So I spread out my big map of Greater Cleveland, outlined every east side suburb, and wrote down the phone numbers of their civil service secretaries. Every six months, I called each one to check on upcoming police exams.

This was going to take time. But I was ready.

***

At first, I planned to focus on my book about working for Sammy Davis, Jr., but as I uncovered more about my grandfather's murder, that story pulled me in instead. I packed my notes and memorabilia into a box labeled "SAMMY" and stored it in a closet. Then, armed with the exact date of my grandfather's death, I went to the public library to search their newspaper archives.

The librarian brought me a microfilm reel of *The Plain Dealer* and patiently showed me how to use the viewing machine to select images and print copies. Turning the hand crank, I fast-forwarded to February 25, 1932, not knowing what to expect—a brief article, a detailed report, or maybe nothing at all. Then, I was stunned to see the front-page headline.

GANG GUNS KILL TWO PORRELLOS AND ALLY

The story ran on pages two and three. It had grainy photos and smaller related articles. I was captivated.

On a frigid afternoon in February 1932, my grandfather, one of his brothers, and their bodyguard played cards in a dingy cigar and soda shop on Cleveland's east side. A coal stove warmed the room. Overhead, two songbirds in separate cages flitted and chirped. The card players were focused on their hands when the front door burst open. Three men with pistols opened fire. The murders of my grandfather, uncle, and their bodyguard brought an end to the so-called "Sugar War" over control of corn sugar. It had been a lucrative Prohibition-era commodity stained with the blood of ambitious but ill-guided men.

What a story! My relatives figured prominently in the beginning of the Italian-American Mafia in Cleveland. It was nothing to be proud of, but it was a fascinating, if dark, slice of national crime history. My father didn't share my curiosity. He spoke little of this painful history. His overarching childhood recollection was of "turmoil."

Through my research, I realized the story was big and complex. The more I learned, the more I knew it had to be a book. And who better to research and write the story than the grandson and nephew of the principal characters?

I spoke with my father. "Dad, I want to write a book about it."

"Leave it alone," he said. His warning, suggestive but forceful, made me hesitate, but my curiosity wouldn't let go.

I began writing, knowing I'd likely disappoint my father again.

I developed a penchant for investigating. Library resources in Cleveland and Cuyahoga County were invaluable as I ferreted out newspaper and magazine articles. I interviewed an assortment of old-timers who recalled bits and pieces of the story. As I obtained photographs and showed my father, his disapproval waned, bringing me both relief and encouragement.

Dad helped fill in details he remembered or later learned as a young adult. In one heart-wrenching story, he recalled being just six years old, right near the cigar shop when his father and uncle were murdered. A family friend had taken him to buy candy. When the shots rang out nearby, the man quickly realized what had happened. He scooped up my father and rushed him to the Porrello house, yelling, "They got Raymond! They got Raymond!"

Dad told me how, during the crowded wake, he climbed onto the kneeler beside the casket to see his father's lifeless face. That image stayed with me long after our talk—etched in my mind as a haunting reminder of the violence and bloodshed that shadowed my family's past.

***

I used most of the money I saved on the road as a down payment for a single-family home. My father helped me paint and make some repairs before I rented it out to a young married couple. By now, it had been one and a half years since I left Sammy's show. I had taken about eight police entrance exams. My scores had risen to the high eighties—still not good enough to get called in for an interview. I considered returning to music full-time and put a few feelers out. I had one offer to move to Branson, Missouri, an up-and-coming entertainment destination.

More importantly, I wanted to get into the police academy. At the time, a prospective cadet had to be hired or sponsored by a law enforcement agency. I met neither requirement. As an option, I applied for some security jobs. I quickly landed a store detective position with the May Company Department Store. After two weeks of training, I opened the store in the morning, detained shoplifters for the police, helped with employee dishonesty cases, and closed in the evening. The schedule cut into my better-paying drumming gigs. Still, I thought it important to have non-music experience on my resume.

CHAPTER
38

Not long after I left his show, Sammy appeared in *Cannonball Run II*, the 1984 sequel to the wild cross-country race movie. His character was disguised as a police officer. I'd learn later that he was a big fan of *Hill Street Blues*, the gritty cop drama—and one of my favorite television shows. He reportedly ran into the creator once and mentioned his interest in making a cameo as a detective. The appearance never happened, but Sammy's interest suggested his admiration for the world of policing. I'd also learn that nine years earlier, he was sworn in as an honorary police chief of a tiny, mostly black town in Oklahoma. He donated $10,000 and two full university scholarships to them as part of a humanitarian and philanthropic effort by several stars to support struggling communities. To me, these revelations echoed what bodyguard Brian Dellow once told me about Mr. D having a passing fascination with police work.

***

I turned down the Branson, Missouri offer. It was a big move and I wasn't ready to give up on my goal of becoming a cop. At Lakeland

Community College on Cleveland's far east side, my criminal justice professor also happened to be the sheriff of a nearby county. He
knew how passionate I was about police work and offered to spon-
sor me for the police academy. I was thrilled and chose the academy
run by the Cleveland Heights Police Department.

I paid for the tuition with the money I'd saved playing drums.
Classes ran from 8:00 a.m. to 4:00 p.m., Monday through Friday.
The academy was just ten minutes from my parents' place, and I
shaved off a minute by taking a shortcut through a residential area.
In hindsight, I should've stayed on the main road.

There were about twenty other guys in the class. The instructors
were tough but made the lessons engaging. We quickly bonded, and
the days flew by as we trained in laws of arrest, search and seizure,
and the use of force.

About halfway through, I mentioned to the academy commander that I was interested in learning more about the murders
of my grandfather and uncles. He suggested I speak to his friend
at the county coroner's office, so he drove me there after class. She
explained how to request public records, and I soon received copies of the files on my grandfather and three of his six brothers, all
murdered.

On the last day of the academy, I was feeling good. I left the
house with a sense of accomplishment, reflecting on the highs and
lows of the past two years. I turned off the main street and onto a
side road, passing small single-family houses with cars parked along
the curb. Suddenly, a loud thud broke my thoughts. I heard it and
felt it, followed by a spray of pink on my windshield.

Did something bounce off my car?

My foot slammed the brake pedal, and the joy of the morning
drained away in an instant. I got out and walked to the back of the
car. Panic hit me. Near a parked car, a boy of about ten was lying
motionless at the curb. Screaming echoed from a distance, growing

louder. It was his mother, running toward him, her voice cracking with fear.

Did I just hit this boy?

I leaned over on the trunk of my car, unable to move or think straight as sirens approached. Paramedics took the boy away in an ambulance. A police officer asked me to write a statement, handing me a form I recognized from class about investigating traffic crashes. I took deep breaths, trying to steady my trembling hands while the officer photographed my car. When I finally calmed down, I wrote my account.

Another officer interviewed the boy's mother, and I noticed her glance toward me. Then the academy commander arrived.

"Are you okay?" he asked.

I told him I hadn't seen the boy. He told me to go home, assuring me he'd look into it and handle the formalities later.

At home, I paced while waiting for the call. I watched my sister through the front window. She washed the blood off my windshield with a garden hose. I was lost in thought, remembering the carefree days with Sammy Davis Jr., when my only concern was showing up at work on time and playing my ass off.

The phone rang, and my heart skipped.

Please don't tell me he's dead.

"Rick, the kid's gonna be okay," the commander said. "He has a broken arm and a concussion, but he's gonna be fine. His mother said he ran into the street after crossing, and there wasn't anything the driver could've done."

He's going to be okay. There was nothing the driver could've done.

Those words were a relief. I thanked the commander and hung up, feeling a weight lift from my chest. I never heard anything more about the incident, but that traumatic memory stayed with me for years. I'd be forever grateful that the boy wasn't hurt worse.

***

Several times after I left the show, trumpeter Fip Ricard called me. In mid-1985, he came to Cleveland for a few days to visit a lady friend. I picked him up from the airport and brought him to our house for dinner. Afterward, I drove him to his hotel.

Months later, the day after Christmas, Fip called again. His tone was somber. It was about George Rhodes—he passed away in his sleep from a heart attack. Shirley woke on Christmas morning to find him gone. I felt as if an uncle had died unexpectedly.

A few days later, Gina called. She'd heard about George's death and just wanted to talk. We reminisced about our time together and working on Sammy's show. We kept in touch, too, maybe once or twice a year. After talking with Gina, I felt a pang of longing. For a fleeting moment, I wanted nothing more than to go back to those days.

***

Over three years had passed since I left Sammy's show. I'd taken eighteen police entrance exams, completed interviews, and passed both the physical and psychological tests. The physical agility tests were easy. The psych exams, though, were another story. The MMPI (Minnesota Multiphasic Personality Inventory) alone had over five hundred questions. Naturally, the safety directors, mayors, and police chiefs were looking for candidates with emotional intelligence—someone who tested well for honesty and integrity. One exam had just one hundred questions, all requiring a simple yes or no answer. Some seemed like traps—at least that's what

I thought.

I enjoy driving fast. Yes or No?

No. Well, yes. No.

After a moment's hesitation, I answered yes. The question said fast—it didn't specify reckless driving. One could enjoy driving fast on a highway. And sometimes, cops need to drive fast.

Another question caught my attention.

I will enjoy having authority over people. Yes or No?

No. Well, yes. No. Only someone impaired would enjoy that, right?

But after thinking it through, I answered yes. Police officers have authority. It's part of the job, and it's what people trust them with.

I never got feedback on my individual answers, but my scores continued to improve. There were follow-up interviews with psychologists, and I braced myself for tough questions about my motivations.

"What made you, a young drummer traveling the world with a legendary entertainer, leave all that to become a cop? You must be psychologically impaired."

The first question came, as I expected. But I answered honestly—about the police radio that sparked my interest and my cousin who was a cop.

I also worried about background checks. Would my family's old connection to the Cleveland Mafia disqualify me? It was decades in the past and never seemed to be an issue.

Around this time, I played a concert with a college jazz band, and I was featured in an extended solo. The performance was recorded, and my father sent Louie Bellson a copy of the cassette tape. A week later, Louie replied with a letter:

"Rick sounds great. Tell him to keep playing."

CHAPTER
39

It finally happened on a spring morning in May 1986. The police chief of a very small Cleveland suburb called me with a part-time job offer. I accepted right away. But just two hours later, the chief of a slightly larger department called with a full-time position. I accepted that, too, and then called the first chief back to explain and rescind my acceptance.

That day, I picked up my police uniform and went straight home to try it on. I stared at myself in the full-length mirror on my closet door, expecting a rush of excitement. Instead, I felt a sting of reality. Memories of myself in a tuxedo, drumsticks in hand, flooded back. I pictured myself surrounded by powerhouse musicians—maybe in Lake Tahoe, Las Vegas, London, or Paris. Sammy was singing and swinging, the audience clapping along. I remembered the red silk handkerchief he gave his band on my first night, calling me a "bitch of a drummer." But that life was gone. My tux hung in a closet, seldom worn, and the handkerchief lay folded in a drawer. I had traded that world for navy blue trousers, a navy blue shirt, and a navy blue tie. Suddenly, I thought of the Baltimore cop's warning—this career change might be tougher than I imagined. Maybe he was right. But

I pressed on.

I was sworn in at a village council meeting, promising before God to serve and protect, uphold the Constitution, and enforce the laws fairly. My dream had come true—I was a cop. This was my first steady job, with a regular paycheck and good benefits.

There was a certain irony to it. Out of the many police departments for which I might have been hired, this village bordered the Front Row. Every shift, I passed the theater Sammy had opened in 1974. As a boy with a camera, I'd stood near the stage while Sammy greeted me with a warm "Hey, little brother" as I snapped his photo. It was also in that theater where I first met him in his dressing room—memories forever linked to my brother's time as his drummer.

After about eighteen months, I got an offer from a larger police department—one I'd taken an exam for nearly two years earlier. My current chief knew I wanted to be a detective and offered to promote me within two years if I stayed. But I wanted more action and better opportunities, so I went with the bigger agency. I rotated through day, evening, and overnight shifts, patrolling streets and never knowing what each day would bring. I loved the unpredictability—responding to calls without knowing the details until I arrived.

Most of my work involved traffic enforcement, investigating crashes, helping stranded motorists, and checking on guests at our small jail. I responded to burglary and robbery alarms—almost all false—and made arrests for DUI and domestic violence.

Back then, training on mental health crises was almost non-existent, but we were getting more calls for help. In the 1980s, mental health facilities closed due to budget cuts and deinstitutionalization. State hospitals shut down, and community services were stretched thin. We weren't therapists, but we were often the only ones available 24/7.

One of my first calls like this came at 1 a.m. on a Sunday in a shopping plaza. A sixteen-year-old boy sat on the curb, threatening suicide with a pocket knife blade pressed to his throat. Three other officers arrived with me. We spoke calmly, trying to get him to put down the knife and go to the hospital. The rescue squad waited nearby. Minutes ticked by—fifteen, thirty, forty-five. The senior officer lit a cigarette, and the boy asked for one. When the officer handed it over, the boy lowered the knife. We all lunged, and in seconds, one officer grabbed the knife and yanked it free. We handcuffed the boy and called paramedics.

One officer spotted my bleeding hand. "Porrello, you're bleeding! What the hell happened?"

I looked down to see a gash on my thumb—small, about an inch, but bleeding fast. A paramedic wrapped it up, and I rode with the boy in the ambulance. The wound needed four stitches.

Back at the station, the teasing started. "Hey, Porrello, didn't they teach you not to grab the blade?"

That little injury earned me three days off. I called Gina and booked a flight to Reno. When I walked out of the jetway into the airport, I daydreamed she'd be waiting, smiling and holding her kangaroo in the air. We met for lunch, and I told her about working as a police officer and how I'd hurt my thumb. She said she'd recently broken up with a boyfriend and was thinking about moving back to Los Angeles. As we talked, I tried to convince myself no time had passed between us—even though I knew it felt like a lifetime ago.

Later, I spent some time at Harrah's, saying hello to a few employees. Doug Bushhausen, the entertainment boss, recognized me and offered to comp me into the evening show. I declined—I wasn't ready for that reminder of the life I'd left behind.

On the flight home, I glanced at my thumb and thought about the risks of police work. It was a small injury, but it made me think of my father. If I were ever killed on duty, he'd lose both a father and a son to violence. That thought haunted me sometimes.

***

I finally completed the last of my required classes to earn my Associate's Degree in Law Enforcement and Criminal Justice. Although it took five years of part-time study, I was proud of the accomplishment.

Juggling a rotating police schedule, I kept playing drums—performing with a lively big band and smaller combos. Ron McCroby, an internationally acclaimed jazz whistler and self-described "puccoloist" from northeast Ohio, often invited me to join him for local concerts and benefit shows. This brought a lot of pride and pleasure to my father, who sometimes came along to my gigs. I loved the applause, the smiles, and the camaraderie with fellow musicians. Even though I occasionally envied those who made music their full-time career, I'd made my choice. I had left that life behind. Sammy Davis, Jr. once joked that I was young enough for seven careers—I hoped to manage just two.

I kept following news about Mr. D, especially after the loss of his longtime conductor, George Rhodes. Sammy brought back Morty Stevens, his first conductor, but after thirty years with George, his professional life was never quite the same.

In 1988, Sammy was honored by the John F. Kennedy Center for the Performing Arts for his lifetime achievement. A few weeks later, he had hip replacement surgery. Then, in 1989, the world learned he had throat cancer. That same year, Sammy released his autobiography, *Why Me*. In September, I watched a televised gala celebrating his sixty years in show business. Hosted by Eddie Murphy, it featured many of Sammy's friends, including Frank Sinatra. A short time after, he received the NAACP Hall of Fame award. Then, on May 16, 1990, Sammy passed away at age sixty-four. As a dramatic tribute, the Las Vegas Strip went dark for ten minutes. The Headliner Room at Harrah's in Reno was renamed Sammy's Showroom. Sammy Davis, Jr. would be remembered as one of the 20th century's greatest entertainers—a true national treasure immortalized in American history.

Meanwhile, in Las Vegas, the casino corporations emerged victorious in a seven-month strike by local Vegas musicians.

As author Janis McKay wrote, "When the corporations decided to cut the hotel bands in favor of synthesizers and [taped music], the rank and file of the union musicians were left behind while the rest of Las Vegas boomed."

Profit was winning out over art—and not just in Vegas. While dinner and cocktail shows at intimate Nevada showrooms served perhaps one thousand guests, sports arenas across the country raked in big money by packing in crowds of twenty thousand.

At home, I witnessed recorded music edging out live music as disc jockeys were popularized for wedding receptions. There was a downward trend in the popularity of jazz, America's music that ironically seemed more popular in Europe and Japan. Count Basie and Buddy Rich were gone. The definition of jazz had broadened over the years, but to me, if it didn't swing, it wasn't jazz. Young luminaries like Wynton Marsalis, Joey DeFrancesco, and Christian McBride rose to stardom. Jazz would survive thanks to passionate students with remarkable talent, supportive parents, seasoned musicians, committed educators, tireless promoters, and loyal fans.

The era of charismatic Rat Pack crooners like Sammy Davis, Jr., Frank Sinatra, and Dean Martin—joking and schmoozing with audiences—was fading. A new kind of glamour was emerging with lavish production shows and their spectacular assault on the senses. Las Vegas found new sources of income from hosting corporate conventions. There would still be live music, but the era of full-time house orchestras in Nevada was nearly over.

Sammy's death compelled me to reflect on my career transition. I was grateful to have worked for him for two and a half years. It felt like I'd just caught the tail end of an era. And it dawned on me that walking away from a budding music career for police work was probably a smart move for my future. Still, I wasn't fully satisfied. I continued playing drums part-time and loved being on stage with the talented musicians I was fortunate to play alongside. But the doubt about forsaking music for law enforcement persisted.

Did I give up too much to become a cop?

I heard about a new book called *When All You've Ever Wanted Isn't Enough*. The title felt like it was aimed right at me.

Yes—when all you've ever wanted isn't enough.

It was written by a rabbi named Harold Kushner. Intrigued, I bought a copy and devoured it within days. The book is grounded in both biblical and practical insights. I was struck by the simplicity with which Rabbi Kushner explains why so many people—despite achieving financial or career success—still feel a sense of dissatisfaction in their lives. He writes about our deep need for meaning and how acts of kindness toward others are never wasted.

It took a few years, but I finally adopted a more positive outlook.

Though I love playing the drums, maybe for me, protecting people is just a little more important than entertaining them.

I found my answer.

The reality of my unlikely career transition—from drummer for a legendary entertainer to cop—hit home when I saw myself in uniform for the first time. 1986.

With Louie Bellson, 1989.

With singers Freddy Cole and Jimmy "Little Jimmy" Scott, who were guests at a Duke Ellington centennial tribute concert in 1999. I was performing with Ernie Krivda's Fat Tuesday Big Band. Other guests included Louie Bellson, Eric Reed, and David Sanborn.

With the amazing jazz whistler Ron McCroby and my father.

One of my favorite photographs—my brother Ray and I
with Sammy—Caesars Palace, Las Vegas, 1981.

EPILOGUE

I might've listened to my father if I'd known just how long it would take to research and write about my grandfather. By 1993, I was already married and had been working for six years on my book about the Cleveland Mafia, trying to understand the bigger picture behind the murders of my grandfather and three uncles. I was almost done and starting to send proposals to publishers. After two years of rejection letters, I swore I'd never write another book.

Then, in 1994, Barricade Books came through with a contract. A year later, *The Rise and Fall of the Cleveland Mafia* hit the shelves. When I held that first hardcover copy, I knew I wanted to write another book. I finished *To Kill the Irishman*—about racketeer Danny "The Irishman" Greene—a few years later and self-published it. Even before it officially hit the shelves, a producer reached out about the film rights. I signed with an agent, and the book was optioned, but the development process dragged on for years.

As usual, Louie Bellson and my father kept in touch. We always got together with Louie when he played in Cleveland. In 1999, I had the honor of playing in a "drum battle" with him. He was in his mid-seventies but still sounded incredible. That same year, I was promoted to sergeant. My father was there for the ceremony, watching my wife pin my first gold badge to my uniform. He died before

I received my final promotion. I wish he could've been there, but I knew he was proud.

By then, a few biographies about Sammy had been published, revealing the toll that overspending and poor investment advice had taken. Still, his remarkable legacy—in music, entertainment, and civil rights—lives on.

In 2011, *Kill the Irishman* finally hit theaters, with Ray Stevenson in the lead role and an outstanding supporting cast. Gina, now married with kids, called to congratulate me. She had since left Vegas, moved back to Los Angeles, become a real estate agent, and kept playing music. We spoke every couple of years—always friendly—even though our lives had taken different paths.

Over the years, I've often pulled out that box of memories—programs, photos, and itineraries from my time with Sammy. Sometimes I wonder what would've happened if I'd stayed in music. But I've come to believe that life tends to take you where you need to be the most.

Looking back on my journey—music, my time protecting and serving, the books I've written, and family—I never chased success, but I've been blessed with more than I ever imagined. And for that, I'm grateful.

DEAR READER

Dear Reader,

Thank you for choosing to read my memoir. Writing this book has been a deeply personal and time-consuming journey, and I hope you found it meaningful. If you enjoyed it, I'd truly value a review.

Your honest feedback not only helps me to improve as a writer—it also helps others discover the story.

You can share your thoughts on Amazon, Goodreads, Barnes & Noble, Facebook, or simply by recommending it to friends and family. Every review or personal recommendation makes a difference, and your support means a great deal.

With appreciation,

Rick Porrello

ABOUT THE AUTHOR

Photo by Rebecca Bihun

Rick Porrello is a musician, and former police chief with deep ties to Italian-American Mafia history. His first book, *The Rise and Fall of the Cleveland Mafia*, grew out of a personal investigation into the unsolved murders of his grandfather and three uncles—mob leaders during Prohibition. That connection sparked a broader exploration of Cleveland's organized crime history.

His second book, the self-published *To Kill the Irishman*,

was adapted into the 2011 film *Kill the Irishman*, starring Ray Stevenson. He has since authored several other books on organized crime including *There's More Bodies Out There: The True Story of a Mafia Associate and a Cop Who Emerge As Suspected Serial Killers.*

Rick enjoyed a 33-year career in law enforcement, including ten years as police chief of a Cleveland, Ohio suburb. Before entering the field, he was a successful jazz drummer who toured for two and a half years with Sammy Davis, Jr.—an experience that inspired his memoir, *Just Play Like You Do in the Basement: Coming of Age as the Drummer for the Greatest Entertainer in the World.*

He currently has multiple book and film projects in development.

www.rickporrello.com

FEATURED TITLES BY RICK PORRELLO

The Rise and Fall of the Cleveland Mafia: Corn Sugar and Blood
(Next Hat Press, 2023)

This enduring chronicle, originally published in 1995, is based on the author's research into the murders of his grandfather and three uncles. The Porrello and Lonardo families, childhood friends in Sicily, dominated the corn sugar trade during Prohibition, when liquor was outlawed. After a rogue Porrello employee sparked the bloody Sugar War, Angelo "Big Ange" Lonardo committed a high-profile murder, securing his place in the crime family.

The Porrello family's attempt to solidify power through the first national meeting of the Sicilian-American Mafia failed. The Mayfield Road mob, with their Jewish allies, took over, ranking third in power after the New York and Chicago families.

The Cleveland Mafia maintained influence and wealth through labor union racketeering and skimming Las Vegas casino profits. The bosses kept a low profile until Danny "The Irishman" Greene rose to power after the 1975 murder of Alex "Shondor" Birns. Greene was eliminated, but the group's troubles worsened when they partnered with drug ring leader Carmen Zagaria. Law enforcement wreaked havoc on the organization, aided by two surprising defections. The fallout spread into several high-profile cases.

There's More Bodies Out There: The True Story of a Mafia Associate and a Cop Who Emerge as Suspected Serial Killers (Next Hat Press, LLC, 2023)

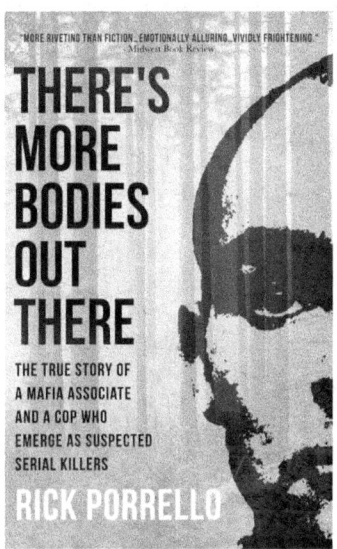

Under a veneer of normalcy lurks the true Richard Henkel. Federal parole authorities deemed the incarcerated bank robber psychologically stable and ready to contribute to society. They were wrong. Henkel thrived in the 1970s underworld—a loose network of drug dealers, burglars, pimps, and Mafia members in Pittsburgh and Youngstown, Ohio. His crew, including convicted killer Jack Siggson and Vietnam vet-turned-cop Gary Small, found him loyal. Dick would never rat out a pal—though he might kill him. Or her.

Henkel was connected to massage parlor "rub and tug" sex shops, which politicians struggled to regulate and mobsters fought to control.

From murders for profit to a plot to kidnap a wealthy businessman, Henkel's actions made headlines. His victims were numerous but never random. He wasn't the typical serial killer, driven by twisted pleasure or power. His targets often had their own sins.

Intensified by ten months of questioning Henkel, *There's More Bodies Out There* reveals the maddening story of one of the most dangerous con artists in U.S. history, his victims, and the lawmen who worked to uncover the truth and serve justice.

NOTES

Chapter 2

p. 8   Photographs of musicians and bands: The bands included pop-
        ular groups led by my cousins Joey Porrello, and Art Porrello.

p. 9   Nationally recognized percussion instructors: Henry Adler
        and Charles Wilcoxon. Ray's studies continued with Bob
        McKee, drummer for Cleveland's Theatrical Grille house
        band and the Mike Douglas TV show.

p. 13   The Local 4 president: Tony Granata. The secretary-treasurer:
        Mike Scigliano.

Chapter 4

p. 20   An arts center: This was the Fairmount Center for the Arts in
        Russell Twp., OH

p. 21   My brother's new career was taking him on short tours with
        nationally known performers: They included pianists Roger
        Williams and Carmen Cavallaro, and actress Totie Fields.

p. 21   Redd Foxx had a singer and another comedian on his show.
        The singer was Talya Ferro and the comedian was Slappy
        White.

Chapter 5

p. 28   A young nun: Sr. Gretchen Rodenfels, OSU.

Chapter 6

p. 32   Cleveland's mayor: Ralph Perk.

p. 33   "mutual adoration" *Between You and Me*. (P. Bailey).

p. 33   "I had to hit the ball" *Backstage at the Tonight Show*. (D.

Sweeney).

p. 34   In late 1974, Count Basie was searching for a new drummer: Basie's previous drummers included jazz greats Joe "Papa Joe" Jones, Sonny Payne, and Rufus "Speedy" Jones.

Chapter 8

p. 39   My brother, Ray Porrello, Jr., replaced the ever-smiling and high-energy drummer Duffy Jackson who had worked for Sammy two years. Previous long-term stickmen included Del Blake and Sammy's first drummer, Michael Silva.

p. 40   "The greatest juvenile entertainer in the world." *Waterbury Democrat*, April 3, 1931.

p. 40   Sammy and his father tried to enlist: *Yes I Can* (S. Davis and Boyar).

p. 40   He was annoyed: *Yes I Can* (S. Davis and Boyar).

p. 41   "touching their emotions" *Why Me* (S. Davis and Boyar).

p. 41   "Sergeant Williams was my savior." *Sammy Davis, Jr.* (T. Davis).

p. 41   "Frank took me under his wing." *Yes I Can* (S. Davis and Boyar).

p. 42   "It's not a colored act." *Yes I Can* (S. Davis and Boyar).

p. 43   He admired the Jewish people's history: *These Are a Swinging Bunch of People* (R. Davis).

p. 43   Judaism provided the spiritual strength: *Why I Became a Jew.* (T. Feldman).

p. 43   "king of the nightclubs." *Nevada State Journal,* August 29, 1959.

p. 43   He helped to desegregate Las Vegas: The Sands president was Jack Entratter.

p. 44   "You is black. But you don't be black." *Why Me.* (S. Davis and Boyar).

Chapter 9

p. 45   Sammy and Company TV Show: Other repeat guests included Lola Falana, Freddie Prinze, Ben Vereen, Totie Fields, and Charo.

p. 45   An all-star big band: George Rhodes directed the Sammy and Co. All Stars which included tenor saxophonist Herman Riley, trumpeters Bobby Bryant and Harry "Sweets" Edison, trombonist Kai Winding, pianist Paul Smith, and bassist Al McKibbon.

Chapter 10

p. 49   Cleveland Heights High School band directors: Bob Bergantino and Jim Bane.

p. 51   My father referred me to a local trumpeter: Lou Sivillo.

p. 53   The owner, the contest host: Joe Matcsak.

p. 55   The regional competition: The contest host was Capital University's percussion director Bob Breithaupt.

p. 57   Jack Sheldon's all-star jazz combo: The band included Jimmy Cleveland on trombone, Mundell Lowe on guitar and Ray Brown on bass.

p. 58   Well-known music professors and performers: The other drum contest judges were Leonard DiMuzio from the Avedis Zildjian Co.; Dr. William Foster, director of bands at Florida A&M University; Dr. William Fowler, a professor of music at the University of Colorado at Denver; George Gaber, a professor of music at Indiana University; and Tony Papa, vice president at Associated Booking Corporation.

p. 58-59   The evening started with an introduction by the host, the university's band director, then comments by the president of the Slingerland: They were Charles A. Lee and Larry R. Linkin. Slingerland's contest director was Sam Geati.

Chapter 14

p. 85   Sammy's previous bassist: Al McKibbon.

Chapter 15

p. 93   Charles "Mickey" Laverine: Mickey had worked previously for Sammy and most recently replaced pianist Rudi Eagan.

p. 97   Sticking Together: *Plain Dealer,* January 29, 1981 (M. Ward.)

Chapter 17

p. 113   Sammy frequently performed at Caesars Palace: The orchestra contractor was Al Ramsey.

p. 114   A local reporter wrote about me and Ray: This is Las Vegas, April 17, 1981 (L. Patterson).

p. 115   Gangsters wowed Sammy: *In Black and White* (W. Haygood).

p. 116   In return, [Sammy] would have to pay. *Gonna Do Great Things.* (G. Fishgall)

p. 116   [Sammy] wanted to throw money. *In Black and White.* (W. Haygood).

Chapter 18

p. 120   Harrah's Reno and Lake Tahoe house orchestras were given one night off each week and were replaced by a relief band led by Johnny Russell. The house bands for Reno and Lake Tahoe were led by John Carlton and Brian Farnon, respectively.

p. 125   George played piano for numerous well-known jazz artists: They included Lil Green, Red Allen, Arnett Cobb and J.C. Higginbotham.

Chapter 19

p. 127   *I've Gotta Be Me*: Music and lyrics by Walter Marks. (ASCAP)

p. 128   *The Candy Man*: Music and lyrics by Leslie Bricusse and Anthony Newley. (BMI)

p. 129   *Sing, Sing, Sing*: written by Louis Prima. (ASCAP)

p. 129   *Night and Day*: Cole Porter. (ASCAP)

Chapter 20

p. 135   Two Cleveland labor union officials: Alfred Antenucci and Frank J. McNamara.

Chapter 21

p. 139   "next to the mixed nuts" *Sammy: An Autobiography*. (S. Davis and Boyar).

p. 139-140 I was never in his house: *Sammy: Peace & Love*. Documentary. Dir. by Ron Joy.
The Lavish Life of Sammy Davis. (R. Mann, Memphis Press-Scimitar).
It's Got to be His. (P. Slansky, Daily News).
Lunch at Sammy's House. (W. Fanning, Pittsburgh Post-Gazette).

p. 141   "I hope the sauce turns out." *Sammy: Peace & Love*. Documentary. Dir. by Ron Joy.

Chapter 23

p. 152   I learned that years earlier, Holmes: Interview with Matthew Hendricksen, 2024.

p. 154   "With a metal detector" *Minneapolis Star Tribune*, Jan. 19, 1981.

p. 155   I asked the house percussionist about her: Mark Barnett.

p. 155   *Mr. Bojangles*: Jerry Jeff Walker (BMI)

Chapter 24

p. 163   *The Birth of the Blues*: Music by Ray Henderson and lyrics by Buddy DeSylva and Lew Brown. Public domain.

Chapter 25

p. 178   *I Can Do That*: Music by Marvin Hamlisch and lyrics by Edward Kleban. (BMI / ASCAP)

p. 179   Billy Preston was with us again: His drummer was Paul Hines.

p. 180   *Peter, Paul and Mary*: Peter Yarrow, Paul Stookey and Mary Travers.

Chapter 27

p. 192   I knew he'd have the house drummer cover: He was Gerry Genuario.

Chapter 30

p. 213   "Get rid of whoever he's got with him." *In Black and White*. (W. Haygood).

Chapter 31

p. 221   Basie and his rhythm section: The bassist was Cleveland Eaton and, of course, Freddie Green was the guitarist. Butch Miles was no longer the drummer, having been replaced by Gregg Fields.

p. 221   *Ding Dong! The Witch is Dead*: Music by Harold Arlen and lyrics by E.Y. Harburg. (ASCAP)

Chapter 33

p. 239   Frank Sinatra's musicians: During my time with Sammy, Frank's pianist/conductor was Vinny Falcone.

p. 239   ... was a former Secret Service agent: Ken Delahunt.

Chapter 34

p. 242   Two friends from home: Rick Veccia and Tom Inck

Chapter 36

p. 255   Ray had recently been hired as the drummer for Caesars Palace: He replaced Joey Preston.

p. 256   "Star policy" Played *Out on the Strip*. (J. McKay).

p. 256   "You're looking at a dinosaur" Interview with former Las Vegas musician Linda Metaxas-Fisher, 2024.

p. 257   *Pagliacci*: Composed by Ruggero Leoncavallo.

p. 257   *Carmen Jones*: The play *Carmen* was written by Prosper Mérimée, a French novelist and dramatist, and first published in 1845 as a novella. Georges Bizet composed the iconic opera adaptation, which premiered in 1875, based on Mérimée's work. *Carmen Jones*, an African-American adaptation, was written by Oscar Hammerstein II.

Chapter 38

p. 269   Sammy and *Hill Street Blues*: "15 Surprising Facts About Hill Street Blues" (R. Cormier, Mental Floss, Jan. 15, 2018. https://www.mentalfloss.com/article/73436/, accessed June 28, 2025

p. 269   Sammy as honorary police chief: This was for the town of Langston, OK. The other honorary police chiefs were Redd Foxx in Taft, OK, and Flip Wilson in Boley, OK. *The Daily Oklahoman* (Oklahoma City) Feb. 25, 1975, and *The Buffalo Grove Herald* (Wheeling, IL) March 4, 1975

p. 270   My criminal justice professor: Jim Todd.

p. 271   The police academy commander: Tim Cannon.

Chapter 39

p. 278   I kept playing drums: I worked with a few small groups, most often those led by Hank Geer or Ernie Krivda, and also performed with Krivda's *Fat Tuesday Big Band*.

BIBLIOGRAPHY

Books

Bailey, Pearl. *Between You and Me*. Doubleday, 1989.

Birkbeck, Matt. *Deconstructing Sammy: Music, Money, Madness, and the Mob*. Amistad, 2008.

Davis, Jr., Sammy, and Jane and Burt Boyar. *Yes I Can*. Farrar, Strauss & Giroux, 1965.

Davis, Jr., Sammy, and Jane and Burt Boyar. *Why Me?* Warner Books, 1989.

Davis, Jr., Sammy, and Jane and Burt Boyar. *Sammy: An Autobiography*. Farrar, Strauss & Giroux, 2000.

Davis, Tracey, and Nina Bunche Pierce. *Sammy Davis Jr.: A Personal History with My Father*. Running Press, 2014.

English, T.J. *Dangerous Rhythms: Jazz and the Underworld*. HarperCollins, 2022.

Fishgall, Gary. *Gonna Do Great Things: the Life of Sammy Davis, Jr.* Scribner, 2003.

Haygood, Wil. *In Black and White: The Life of Sammy Davis, Jr.* Alfred A. Knopf, 2003.

Jacobson, Matthew Frye. *Dancing Down the Barricades: Sammy Davis, Jr. and the Long Civil Rights Era*. University of California Press, 2023.

Kelley, Kitty. *His Way: The Unauthorized Biography of Frank Sinatra*. Bantam Books, 1986.

Kerz, Florian, and Ivar Halstvedt. *Beyond Bojangles: the Sammy Davis, Jr. Encyclopedia*. BOD, Norderstedt, Germany, 2014.

Kushner, Harold. *When All You've Ever Wanted Isn't Enough*. Summit Books, 1986

McKay, Janis. *Played Out on the Strip: the Rise and Fall of Las Vegas Casino Bands*. University of Nevada Press, 2016

Porrello, Rick. *The Rise and Fall of the Cleveland Mafia: Corn Sugar and Blood*. Barricade Books, 1995.

Sherrod, Pamela. *The Last Chapter in the Life of Mrs. Sammy Davis, Jr.* Pamela Sherrod Ministries, 2009.

Sweeney, Don. *Backstage at the Tonight Show: From Johnny Carson to Jay Leno*. Taylor Trade Publishing, 2006.

Documentaries

Sammy: Peace & Love. Directed by Ron Joy. Produced by Carl Axel Hellqvist. A Craven Films Production, 2023. Accessed May 29, 2023. https://www.youtube.com/watch?v=6xba8KAnwVY.

Magazine and Newspaper articles

Davis, Rebecca L. "These Are a Swinging Bunch of People: Sammy Davis, Jr., Religious Conversion, and the Color of Jewish Ethnicity." American Jewish History 100, no. 1, January 2016

Deni, Laura. "A Day in Las Vegas: An MD Special Report on the Louie Bellson National Drum Contest Finals." Modern Drummer, Apr-May 1980.

Fanning, Win. "Lunch at Sammy's House." Pittsburgh Post-Gazette, June 26, 1973.

Feldman, Trude. "Why I Became a Jew: Entertainer Says Judaism Was Answer to 'Life Filled with Confusion.'" Ebony, February 1960.

Mann, Roderick. "The Lavish Life of Sammy Davis." Memphis Press-Scimitar, Feb. 28, 1975.

Slansky, Paul. "It's Got to be His." Daily News. NY. N.Y. Nov. 15, 1981.

Tuber, Keith. "Lounging With the Dae Han Sisters." Orange Coast Magazine, October 1987. Via Google Books: https://tinyurl.com/yccwhy52; accessed 3-27-2025

Newspapers

Beacon Journal (Akron)
Buffalo Grove Herald (Wheeling)
Cincinnati Enquirer
Daily News (NY)
Daily Oklahoman

Evening News (Reno)
Kenosha News
Las Vegas Sun
Memphis Press-Scimitar
Minneapolis Star Tribune
Nevada State Journal
New York Times
Plain Dealer (Cleveland)
Post-Gazette (Pittsburgh)
Reno Gazette-Journal
Waterbury Democrat

Websites

Jerry Lewis & Sammy Davis Jr. - *Move & Come Rain Or Come Shine*, 1981, MDA Telethon. YouTube, uploaded by www.MDA.org. www.youtube.com/watch?v=CH1zhinKmw0. www.MDA.org. Accessed 15 Dec. 2023.

Wikipedia (https://www.wikipedia.org/) — Used occasionally for general background and fact-checking of dates, places, and names.

Recommended reading about Sammy Davis, Jr.

Birkbeck, Matt. *Deconstructing Sammy: Music, Money, Madness, and the Mob*. Amistad, 2008.

Davis, Sammy Jr., and Jane and Burt Boyar. *Why Me?* Warner Books, 1989.

Fishgall, Gary. *Gonna Do Great Things: The Life of Sammy Davis, Jr.* Scribner, 2003.

Haygood, Wil. *In Black and White: The Life of Sammy Davis, Jr.* Alfred A. Knopf, 2003.

Jacobson, Matthew Frye. *Dancing Down the Barricades: Sammy Davis, Jr. and the Long Civil Rights Era*. University of California Press, 2023.

INDEX

www.ingramcontent.com/pod-product-compliance
Lightning Source LLC
Chambersburg PA
CBHW070546130626

46556CB00001B/42